The Holocaust and its Contexts

Series Editors

Ben Barkow
The Holocaust Survivors' Friendship Association
Huddersfield, UK

Suzanne Bardgett
Imperial War Museum
London, UK

More than sixty years on, the Holocaust remains a subject of intense debate with ever-widening ramifications. This series aims to demonstrate the continuing relevance of the Holocaust and related issues in contemporary society, politics and culture; studying the Holocaust and its history broadens our understanding not only of the events themselves but also of their present-day significance. The series acknowledges and responds to the continuing gaps in our knowledge about the events that constituted the Holocaust, the various forms in which the Holocaust has been remembered, interpreted and discussed, and the increasing importance of the Holocaust today to many individuals and communities.

Dan Stone

Psychoanalysis, Historiography, and the Nazi Camps

Accounting for Survival

Dan Stone
Royal Holloway, University of London
London, UK

ISSN 2731-5711　　　　　　　ISSN 2731-572X　(electronic)
The Holocaust and its Contexts
ISBN 978-3-031-58009-3　　　ISBN 978-3-031-58010-9　(eBook)
https://doi.org/10.1007/978-3-031-58010-9

© The Editor(s) (if applicable) and The Author(s), under exclusive license to Springer Nature Switzerland AG 2024
This work is subject to copyright. All rights are solely and exclusively licensed by the Publisher, whether the whole or part of the material is concerned, specifically the rights of translation, reprinting, reuse of illustrations, recitation, broadcasting, reproduction on microfilms or in any other physical way, and transmission or information storage and retrieval, electronic adaptation, computer software, or by similar or dissimilar methodology now known or hereafter developed.
The use of general descriptive names, registered names, trademarks, service marks, etc. in this publication does not imply, even in the absence of a specific statement, that such names are exempt from the relevant protective laws and regulations and therefore free for general use.
The publisher, the authors and the editors are safe to assume that the advice and information in this book are believed to be true and accurate at the date of publication. Neither the publisher nor the authors or the editors give a warranty, expressed or implied, with respect to the material contained herein or for any errors or omissions that may have been made. The publisher remains neutral with regard to jurisdictional claims in published maps and institutional affiliations.

Cover illustration: © Wolfgang Spitzbart / Alamy

This Palgrave Macmillan imprint is published by the registered company Springer Nature Switzerland AG.
The registered company address is: Gewerbestrasse 11, 6330 Cham, Switzerland

Paper in this product is recyclable.

Acknowledgements

My thanks first of all to Éva Kovács and Natalia Aleksiun, organizers of the *Survivors' Toil* conference, held at the Vienna Wiesenthal Institute in November 2022, and to Emily Russell at Palgrave, for encouraging me to pursue this project. Thanks too to those who helped me obtain material: Jason Potter, Dawn Skorczewski, and Simon Sparks. Particular thanks to Ian Rich at the Wiener Holocaust Library, who generously gave of his time to find documents for me. Finally, many thanks to my colleagues with whom I've discussed this project and whose comments have been invaluable: Jan Burzlaff, Paris Chronakis, Bob Eaglestone, Christian Fleck, Florin Lobonț, Stephen Naron, William Pimlott, Lisa Pine, and Christine Schmidt. I'm especially grateful to Sue Vice, Hank Greenspan, and Daniel Pick for reading the text so carefully and for providing insightful comments and corrections.

Contents

1 Introduction: Psychoanalysis, Holocaust Historiography, and Survival ... 1

2 Survival Through Stupor: Eddy de Wind and Early-Postwar Psychoanalytic Studies of the Nazi Concentration Camps ... 19

3 The Female Doctors of Block 10 in Auschwitz: Gender, Resistance, and Survival ... 43

4 Revisiting Survival: Hilde O. Bluhm on Early Accounts of the Nazi Concentration Camps ... 65

5 Conclusion ... 91

Bibliography ... 99

Index ... 115

CHAPTER 1

Introduction: Psychoanalysis, Holocaust Historiography, and Survival

Abstract Here I discuss the main developments in Holocaust historiography and psychoanalytic thought since the end of the war, especially in the ways that they intersect. Noting that psychohistory is (for good reason) unfashionable, I argue nevertheless that both disciplines have much to learn from each other. With respect to the Nazi movement, psychoanalytical vocabulary provides a useful way of engaging with the drives that underpinned Hitler's rise to power and the crimes committed by the Nazi regime. And with respect to surviving the Nazi camps—the main focus here—psychoanalytic explanations offer much food for thought. Although the main factor for survival was luck, inmates struggled on a daily basis to maintain their psychological poise sufficiently to withstand their ill-treatment. When it comes to the postwar psychoanalytical or psychotherapeutic treatment of survivors and, later, their children, the record is mixed and I discuss this history briefly too. But the main focus is on the historiographical debate surrounding the conditions that promoted survival.

Keywords Psychoanalysis • Holocaust • Historiography • Survival

Even if we confine ourselves to the Freudian tradition, psychoanalytic theory has changed enormously over the century or so since its founding. The historiography of the events that since the 1960s have been known as the Holocaust has likewise changed a great deal since it began to be written even before the end of World War II. These two statements are not unrelated.

At first glance, it might seem as if psychoanalysis has been reshaped in the wake of our expanding knowledge and deeper understanding of the Holocaust more than vice-versa. The move away from regarding psychological problems as responses to childhood sexual abuse in a universally applicable psychosexual development in favor of a model in which the psychic illnesses are understood as impacted by events in the external world later in life clearly owes a great deal to, and was in turn defined through, the notion of trauma, for which the Holocaust and other horrific events beginning with World War I have been crucial. The scandal of restitution claims in the 1950s and 1960s was one important waystation in this development: the refusal of West German assessors to recognize that survivors' illnesses were related to their suffering under the Nazis rather than Oedipal problems stemming from their childhood brought about a gradual rethinking of some of the basics of Freudian theory.[1] As Ernest Rapaport put it, condemning the "silliness" of earlier psychosexual arguments in this context: "statements made by psychoanalysts that 'external events', no matter how overwhelming, precipitate a neurosis only when they touch on specific unconscious conflicts need revision so far as the survivors of the camps are concerned."[2] Or later, as Jack Terry noted in 1984, "It is unfortunate that a person's having spent time in concentration camps was not considered to be sufficient reason for him to 'deserve'

---

[1] Milton Kestenberg, "Discriminatory Aspects of the German Indemnification Policy: A Continuation of Persecution", in Martin S. Bergmann and Milton E. Jucovy (eds.), *Generations of the Holocaust* (New York: Columbia University Press, 1990), 62–79; Nathan Durst, "Emotional Wounds that Never Heal", *Jewish Political Studies Review*, 14:3–4 (2002), 119–129; Dagmar Herzog, "The Obscenity of Objectivity: Post-Holocaust Anti-Semitism and the Invention-Discovery of Post-Traumatic Stress Disorder," in Wendy Lower and Lauren Faulkner Rossi (eds.), *Lessons and Legacies, Vol. XII: New Directions in Holocaust Research and Education* (Evanston: Northwestern University Press, 2017), 31–63; Rebecca Clifford, *Survivors: Children's Lives after the Holocaust* (New Haven: Yale University Press, 2020), 154–178.

[2] Ernest A. Rapaport, "Beyond Traumatic Neurosis: A Psychoanalytic Study of Late Reactions to the Concentration Camp Trauma", *International Journal of Psychoanalysis*, 49 (1968), 720, cited in Robert Krell, "Psychiatry and the Holocaust", in Robert Krell and Marc I. Sherman, *Medical and Psychological Effects of Concentration Camps on Holocaust Survivors* (New Brunswick: Transaction Publishers, 1997), 8.

compensation and that proof of impairment of physical or mental efficiency was and still remains a requirement."[3] Wiliam Niederland had already pointed out in 1961 that "As important as early developmental factors for the pathogenetic manifestations of neurotic and psychotic conditions are, they can never be the sole consideration in the psychiatric evaluation of mental disorders in concentration-camp survivors."[4] Even if, as Niederland noted, the existence of such a syndrome as he described among camp survivors ran against "accepted psychoanalytic formulations," he insisted that the force and longevity of the persecution suffered under the Nazis could bring about the sort of psychic changes usually understood to result from internal disturbances.[5]

Even as many émigré analysts remained silent about the effects of Nazi persecution on their own lives, others—including some émigrés—treated Holocaust survivors and their children and came to understand the terrible psychological effects of that persecution. One can make a valid claim that analysts often chose not to grapple with the Holocaust, whether out of a disinclination to call into question the values and fundamental presuppositions of the associations to which they belonged or from fear of how doing so might affect their own psychic well-being and ability to practice. The exodus from Nazi-occupied Europe of large numbers of psychiatrists, psychologists, and psychoanalysts and what happened to their relatives who remained behind, is not unrelated to their reluctance to deal with the topic.[6] Nevertheless, compared with other disciplines, such as sociology, anthropology, or political science, in fact psychoanalysts were among the first both before and after 1945 to discuss fascism, Nazism, and the Holocaust (not yet called by that name, of course), or at least certain aspects of it.[7] Post-traumatic stress disorder (PTSD), which many critics

---

[3] Jack Terry, "The Damaging Effects of the 'Survivor Syndrome'", in Steven A. Luel and Paul Marcus (eds.), *Psychoanalytic Reflections on the Holocaust: Selected Essays* (New York: Ktav Publishing House, 1984), 136.
[4] William G. Niederland, "The Problem of the Survivor", *Journal of the Hillside Hospital*, 10:3–4 (1961), 236.
[5] Niederland, "The Problem of the Survivor", 239.
[6] See Robert Krell's incisive opening remarks in "Psychiatry and the Holocaust", 3–22; and Ilse Grubrich-Simitis, "From Concretism to Metaphor: Thoughts on Some Theoretical and Technical Aspects of the Psychoanalytic Work with Children of Holocaust Survivors", *The Psychoanalytic Study of the Child*, 39 (1984), 301–319, where she talks of the "joint acceptance of the Holocaust reality" between analyst and analysand as the necessary prerequisite for successful clinical work.
[7] See, for example, David James Fisher, "Towards a Psychoanalytic Understanding of Fascism and Anti-Semitism: Perceptions from the 1940s", *Psychoanalysis and History*, 6:1 (2004), 57–74.

agree emerged out of "concentration camp survivor syndrome," was, as Andreas Hamburger reminds us, the only category of mental illness defined by an external event when it was introduced to the DSM-III (American Psychiatric Association's *Diagnostic and Statistical Manual of Mental Disorders*) in 1980.[8] If PTSD has taken on a universalist hue that occludes the specificity of the events and subsequent illnesses that first gave rise to its recognition, there is still no doubt that psychoanalysis has responded to the Holocaust. If we add in psychoanalytic approaches to the perpetrators, from Adorno's extraordinary essay on "Freudian theory and the pattern of fascist propaganda" (1951) which talks of "socialized hypnosis," lending support to Leo Lowenthal's notion of fascism as "psychoanalysis in reverse," to the Mitscherlichs' study of postwar German society, to studies of the Goering Institute and the many social-psychological analyses of perpetrators and their descendants, we see an impressive attempt to grapple with Nazism and the Holocaust by psychoanalysts and historians of psychoanalysis.[9] This extends to the question of the intergenerational transmission of unmourned traumas, as Eric Santner notes, following the Mitscherlichs, "the second generation inherited not only the unmourned traumas of the parents but also the psychic structures that impeded mourning in the older generation in the first place."[10]

---

[8] Andreas Hamburger, "Genocidal Trauma: Individual and Social Consequences of Assault on the Mental and Physical Life of a Group", in Dori Laub and Andreas Hamburger (eds.), *Psychoanalysis and Holocaust Testimony: Unwanted Memories of Social Trauma* (London: Routledge, 2017), 83.

[9] See, for example, Matt ffytche, "Psychoanalytic Sociology and the Traumas of History: Alexander Mitscherlich between the Disciplines", *History of the Human Sciences*, 30:5 (2017), 3–29; Theodor W. Adorno, "Freudian Theory and the Pattern of Fascist Propaganda", in Adorno, *The Culture Industry: Selected Essays on Mass Culture*, ed. J. M. Bernstein (London: Routledge, 2001), 132–157; Geoffrey Cocks, *Psychotherapy in the Third Reich: The Goering Institute* (New York: Oxford University Press, 1984); and, most recently, Federico Finchelstein, *Fascist Mythologies: The History and Politics of Unreason in Borges, Freud, and Schmitt* (New York: Columbia University Press, 2022) and Era A. Loewenstein, "In Dark Times: Psychoanalytic Praxis as a Form of Resistance to Fascist Propaganda", *Psychoanalytic Inquiry*, 43:2 (2023), 130–144. More experimental, challenging work can be found in: Klaus Theweleit, *Male Fantasies*, 2 vols., trans. Stephen Conway (Minneapolis: University of Minnesota Press, 1987/1989); Laurance A. Rickels, *Nazi Psychoanalysis*, 3 vols. (Minneapolis: University of Minnesota Press, 2002).

[10] Eric L. Santner, *Stranded Objects: Mourning, Memory, and Film in Postwar Germany* (Ithaca: Cornell University Press, 1990), 37. More broadly, see Werner Bohleber, "Problems in German Remembrance", in Ira Brenner (ed.), *The Handbook of Psychoanalytic Holocaust Studies: International Perspectives* (London: Routledge, 2020), 129–142, and Karl Figlio, *Remembering as Reparation: Psychoanalysis and Historical Memory* (London: Palgrave Macmillan, 2017).

Beyond the focus on Nazism, psychoanalysts have also begun, especially in the wake of the Black Lives Matter movement and broader discussions about decolonization, to tackle questions of the discipline's own Eurocentric assumptions as well as revisiting the topic of racism, which has been a mainstay of concerns for decades.[11]

What of historiography? Psychohistory, which flourished briefly in the 1970s, has long been unfashionable, although during its brief heyday studies of Hitler and anti-Semitism were among its main concerns, especially in the work of Peter Loewenberg.[12] Even though it is not a journal of psychohistory, the journal *Psychoanalysis and History* is decidedly niche today. Historians tend to value empirical details, not theoretical speculation, and they distrust approaches to world historical phenomena, such as the Holocaust, that derive from theories about individuals' unconscious thought processes. Nor do they ordinarily want to apply theories about the individual to groups, political movements or whole societies, as if these have a collective unconscious. As Saul Friedländer noted in his 1975 inquiry into psychohistory: "certain cases present limits that the biographer cannot hope to go beyond. One can define an unconscious structure, both in its typical and its specific characteristics, *but its genesis is sometimes inaccessible to historical study.*"[13] Yet, it is also hard to escape the idea common to the historiography, that with Nazism and the Holocaust something about the phenomena eludes rational understanding. The genocide of the Jews is an archetypal example of unconscious fears and fantasies being enacted on a real-world stage; indeed, it is perhaps the prime example of world events being directed

---

[11] See, for example, Todd McGowan, *The Racist Fantasy: Unconscious Roots of Hatred* (London: Bloomsbury, 2022); Stephen Frosh, *Antisemitism and Racism: Ethical Challenges for Psychoanalysis* (London: Bloomsbury, 2023).

[12] See, for example, Peter Loewenberg, "The Unsuccessful Adolescence of Heinrich Himmler", *American Historical Review*, 76:3 (1971), 612–641; Loewenberg, "The Psychohistorical Origins of the Nazi Youth Cohort", *American Historical Review*, 76:5 (1971), 1457–1502; Saul Friedländer, *L'Antisémitisme nazi: histoire d'une psychose collective* (Paris: Seuil, 1971); Friedländer, *History and Psychoanalysis: An Inquiry into the Possibilities and Limits of Psychohistory*, trans. Susan Suleiman (New York: Holmes & Meier, 1980), 45–48; Pierre Ayçoberry, *The Nazi Question: An Essay on the Interpretations of National Socialism (1922–1975)* (London: Routledge & Kegan Paul, 1981), 180–191. Earlier models for this sort of psychoanalytic Study* (New York: International Universities Press, 1952); Adolf Leschnitzer, *The Magic Background of Modern Anti-Semitism: An Analysis of the German-Jewish Relationship* (New York: International Universities Press, 1956).

[13] Friedländer, *History and Psychoanalysis*, 48. See also Sidney M. Bolkosky, *Searching for Meaning in the Holocaust* (Westport, CT: Greenwood Press, 2002), 8–9.

and shaped by such fears and fantasies.[14] Émigré writer Sebastian Haffner was not the only one to make this point, although he did so with especial clarity and bite in 1940: "to tabulate Hitler, as it were, in the History of Ideas and to degrade him to an historical episode is a hopeless undertaking, and can only lead to perilous miscalculations. Much more progress towards an accurate estimation of the man can be made if one takes exactly the opposite course and considers German and European history as a part of Hitler's private life."[15] Although few historians have followed Wilhelm Reich, Erich Fromm, or Klaus Theweleit to consider Nazism and Nazi perpetrators in light of psychoanalysis in recent years, there are a few exceptions, the most important being Amos Goldberg's *Trauma in First Person* (2017). Employing a combination of psychoanalytical concepts, primarily trauma, with a literary analysis of the diaries of Victor Klemperer, Chaim Kaplan, and others, Goldberg brings to light the workings of what he calls the "helpless consciousness" during the Holocaust. At the same time, he offers a reading of Nazism that equates Nazi law with sadism, that is, the reduction of the Jews to nothingness in order to reassert Aryan sovereignty, leaving the Nazis in the position of the "obscene father-of-enjoyment" taking pleasure in his victims' suffering, and the Jews in the ghetto reduced to internalizing these views about themselves, causing "numbness and internal death."[16]

There is not the space here to go into detail on the course of Holocaust historiography since the end of the war. Suffice it to say that, on the one hand, psychoanalysis has had little direct effect on how historians approach the Holocaust, although terms derived from psychoanalysis such as "trauma," "repetition," and "fantasy" are common and there is a general sense of the Holocaust as a topic that defies understanding. But by comparison with scholars in literature or cultural studies, for example,

---

[14] See Michael Roper, "Psychoanalysis and the Making of History", in Nancy Partner and Sarah R I. Foot (eds.), *The Sage Handbook of Historical Theory* (London: Sage, 2013), 311–325; T. G. Ashplant, "Psychoanalysis in Historical Writing", *History Workshop*, 26 (1988), 102–119; Yoav Di-Capua, "Trauma and Other Historians—An Introduction", *Historical Reflections/Réflexions Historiques*, 41:3 (2015), 1–13.

[15] Sebastian Haffner, *Germany Jekyll and Hyde: An Eyewitness Analysis of Nazi Germany* (London: Libris, 2005), 5.

[16] Amos Goldberg, *Trauma in First Person: Diary Writing during the Holocaust* (Bloomington: Indiana University Press, 2017), xi, 198, and 62. See also Jean-Gérard Bursztein, *Nazisme et Shoah: Une approche psychanalytique* (Paris: Hermann, 2010), esp. ch9: "Le meurtre de masse des Juifs comme victoire du délire", where Bursztein writes (88), in Lacanian fashion, that "the Jews were and still are virtually the carriers of the function of the object a) in the phantasy [*le fantasme*] of European peoples and in certain Islamist discourses."

psychoanalysis does not show up explicitly. In memory studies especially, psychoanalytic concepts such as repression are common, and much of this literature has to do with the Holocaust. On the other hand, Holocaust historians are much more diverse in terms of gender and background than was the case just ten years ago, and the openness to methodological diversity is striking.[17] Where there is a clear influence of psychoanalysis on historical approaches, it tends to be in the work of feminist scholars, such as Karyn Ball and Carolyn Dean, or in the history of psychoanalysis as practiced by historians such as Daniel Pick, Dagmar Herzog, or Rebecca Clifford.

This book does not systematically chart developments in either psychoanalysis or Holocaust historiography.[18] Rather it shows how one specific problem from the Holocaust—that of survival—has exercised both psychoanalysts and historians since 1945 (and in some cases earlier), and how their theories have been and continue to be rethought in light of new knowledge from the archives, the rediscovery of older publications leading to new interpretations, and changes in the wider world which continue to reshape and will always reshape the ways in which scholars of all disciplines approach the past. But rather than giving an overview of psychoanalytic theories, the book focuses on the problem of survival as it is dealt with in the work of specific individual psychoanalysts and medics who survived the Nazi camps or who left Europe as émigrés and who wrote about their own and others' experiences, treated other survivors and then wrote about their therapeutic practice.[19]

* * *

[17] For more detail, see my "The Historiography of the Holocaust: The Years of Diversification and Integration", in Mark Roseman and Dan Stone (eds.), *The Cambridge History of the Holocaust*, Vol. 1 (Cambridge: Cambridge University Press, 2025), and "The Two Faces of the 'Final Solution': Popular Holocaust Memory and Holocaust Historiography", in Wulf Kansteiner and Christina Morina (eds.), *The Oxford Handbook of History and Memory* (Oxford: Oxford University Press, 2024).

[18] For examples of each, see: Stephen A. Mitchell and Margaret J. Black (eds.), *Freud and Beyond: A History of Modern Psychoanalytic Thought* (New York: Basic Books, 1995); Paul Roazen, *The Historiography of Psychoanalysis* (London: Routledge, 2001); Dan Stone, *Histories of the Holocaust* (Oxford: Oxford University Press, 2010); Tom Lawson, *Debates on the Holocaust* (Manchester: Manchester University Press, 2010).

[19] For a much larger, pathbreaking work that brings together history, psychoanalysis and social psychology, using as its source base the reports of surviving psychoanalysts, see Frank Wiedemann, *Psychologen im Konzentrationslager—Methoden und Strategien des Überlebens* (Frankfurt am Main: Peter Lang, 2017). Wiedemann focuses on Ernst Federn, Viktor Frankl, Ella Lingens, and Louis Tas.

According to Henry Krystal and William G. Niederland, "A generalization might be made here that mankind tends to sanctify and adore martyrs but condemns, suspects, or at least ignores survivors."[20] Given the length of time it took for Holocaust survivors to be treated by analysts as people whose experiences challenged psychoanalytical assumptions, and given the suddenness with which Holocaust survivors turned from being ignored to becoming cultural icons (a process not without a whole set of other problems), we might be forgiven for thinking that there is some truth to Krystal and Niederland's claim. Yet, a few years after they wrote these words—only just more than 20 years after the end of the war—the tide was changing. In an important symposium that took place in the early 1980s, psychoanalyst Sidney Furst wrote that:

> In psychoanalytic theory the main focus has been on the intrapsychic effect of trauma, such that in infantile trauma, the weak ego of the child is faced with a problem that the infantile apparatus can't handle, leading to repression and other defenses which affect the total personality. The Holocaust, however, was a massive psychic trauma which distinguished itself not only from infantile trauma but also from war neurosis and battle trauma, because of the duration and intensity of the external stimuli. Therefore, even the strongest ego will fail to protect the psychic apparatus from being traumatized. In terms of technique the notion of bringing the repressed to consciousness with a now more highly developed and better equipped ego, as in the case of an infantile trauma, is not applicable to the Holocaust-induced trauma.[21]

I cannot discuss the question of therapeutic technique, as that is beyond my competence. Analysts have debated the role of transference and counter-transference, as in Dominick LaCapra's insights that historians need to be aware of their own subjectivity and the risks of aestheticizing trauma.[22] They have also explained the need to go beyond mere retelling

---

[20] H. Krystal and W. G. Niederland, "Clinical Observations on the Survivor Syndrome", in Henry Krystal (ed.), *Massive Psychic Trauma* (New York: International Universities Press, 1968), 343. Other psychoanalysts whose work was important in leading to the "discovery" of trauma include Hans Keilson, Hilel Klein, Leo Eitinger, Paul Chodoff, Anna Ornstein, Editha Sterba, and Eddy de Wind.

[21] "Psychoanalysis and the Holocaust: A Roundtable", in Luel and Marcus (eds.), *Psychoanalytic Reflections on the Holocaust*, 211.

[22] See Dominick LaCapra, *Writing History, Writing Trauma* (Baltimore: Johns Hopkins University Press, 2001), esp. ch6.

so as to historicize the trauma in a way that makes the patient recognize its reality—as opposed to it remaining in the realm of fantasy.[23] However, the main issue of importance identified here by Furst is the fact of Holocaust trauma being caused by massive external stimuli. This might seem obvious and uncontentious today, but that was by no means the case in the first few decades after the war. As Werner Bohleber notes, "The field of psychoanalysis was the inner world of the human being—the unconscious, and unconscious phantasies. For many analysts, the adequate integration of external reality seemed like an intrusion on psychic reality and the meaning of the unconscious."[24] Only after many years of research and clinical work has the sort of statement issued by Furst become routine. And only after considerable struggle, since, as Laurence Kahn says, the "Nazis created a reality far more frightening than any trauma," meaning that "there was no other solution than to deviate from the 'orthodox' position of many analysts," even as this was not an option.[25] At the same time as trauma was introduced to the DSM, a parallel development was taking place: the birth of Holocaust video testimony.

Video testimony, as exemplified by the Fortunoff Archive established by psychoanalyst Dori Laub and literary scholar Geoffrey Hartman in 1979, has a history that runs alongside that of trauma theory—in psychoanalysis as well as in cultural studies, literature, and history. This is perhaps not surprising. Just as Holocaust-related trauma was not the first time that trauma had been observed and theorized by psychoanalysts, so video testimony was not the first time that the testimonies of Holocaust survivors had been taken. Even before the end of the war, historical commissions were being established to record survivors' words, and from the end of the war onwards, new research centers such as the Contemporary Jewish Documentation Centre (Paris), the Jewish Historical Institute (Warsaw), the National Committee for Attending Deportees in Budapest, or the Wiener Library (London) undertook programs of recording survivors'

---

[23] See Werner Bohleber, "Treatment, Trauma, and Catastrophic Reality: A Double Understanding of the 'Too Much' Experience and its Implications for Treatment", in Laub and Hamburger (eds.), *Psychoanalysis and Holocaust Testimony*, 19–31, esp. 24–29. See also Lewis A. Kirshner, "Trauma, the Good Object, and the Symbolic: A Theoretical Integration", *International Journal of Psycho-Analysis*, 75:2 (1994), 235–242.
[24] Bohleber, "Treatment, Trauma, and Catastrophic Reality", 20.
[25] Laurence Kahn, *What Nazism Did to Psychoanalysis* (London: Routledge, 2023), 90.

words.[26] In the cases of David Boder and John Stonehill, wire recorders were used to make the earliest audio recordings of survivors, in DP camps in Western Europe and in the Hotel Marseilles in New York City, the gathering point for new immigrants, respectively. Yet, video testimony allowed insights into the ways in which survivors were traumatized that one does not wholly appreciate through the written or spoken word.[27]

Besides, the video testimony setting is, as some scholars have noticed, not dissimilar from the psychoanalytic setting. Amit Pinchevski notes that the "distinctive genre" of video testimony "could be described as a cross between a television interview, oral history, and a psychoanalytic session."[28] The difference is that whereas the latter is confined to the analyst and the analysand, the former requires the presence of audiovisual equipment in order to facilitate the process of witnessing. "Indeed," writes Pinchevski, "it is for the sake of recording that the testimony dyad came together in the first place."[29] Video testimony has not just accompanied a greater, more sophisticated interest in Holocaust testimony; rather, it birthed it: "The audiovisual bears witness to the crisis of testimony by mediating the

[26] Laura Jockusch, *Collect and Record! Jewish Holocaust Documentation in Early Postwar Europe* (New York: Oxford University Press, 2012); Jason Lustig, *A Time to Gather: Archives and the Control of Jewish Culture* (New York: Oxford University Press, 2022); Mark L. Smith, *The Yiddish Historians and the Struggle for a Jewish History of the Holocaust* (Detroit: Wayne State University Press, 2019); Christine Schmidt, "'We are All Witnesses': Eva Reichmann and the Wiener Library's Eyewitness Accounts Collection", in Thomas Kühne and Mary Jane Rein (eds.), *Agency and the Holocaust: Essays in Honor of Debórah Dwork* (Cham: Palgrave Macmillan, 2020), 123–140.

[27] The classic works are: Lawrence L. Langer, *Holocaust Testimonies: The Ruins of Memory* (New Haven: Yale University Press, 1991); Shoshana Felman and Dori Laub, *Testimony: Crises of Witnessing in Literature, Psychoanalysis, and History* (New York: Routledge, 1992); Henry Greenspan, *On Listening to Holocaust Survivors: Recounting and Life History* (Westport, CT: Praeger, 1998). For more recent work, see inter alia: Thomas Trezise, *Witnessing Witnessing: On the Reception of Holocaust Survivor Testimony* (New York: Fordham University Press, 2013); Noah Shenker, *Reframing Holocaust Testimony* (Bloomington: Indiana University Press, 2015); Jeffrey Shandler, *Holocaust Memory in the Digital Age: Survivors' Stories and New Media Practices* (Stanford: Stanford University Press, 2017); Hannah Pollin-Gallay, *Ecologies of Witnessing: Language, Place, and Holocaust Testimony* (New Haven: Yale University Press, 2018); Steffi de Jong, *The Witness as Object: Video Testimony in Memorial Museums* (Oxford: Berghahn, 2018); Matthew Boswell and Antony Rowland, *Virtual Holocaust Memory* (New York: Oxford University Press, 2023).

[28] Amit Pinchevski, "Counter-testimony, Counter-archive", in Laub and Hamburger (eds.), *Psychoanalysis and Holocaust Testimony*, 242. The proximity of oral history to psychoanalysis has also been noted, but that discussion is beyond the scope of this book.

[29] Pinchevski, "Counter-testimony, Counter-archive", 243.

vacillations of narrative in giving an account of trauma."[30] That is to say, with video testimony one can visualize what trauma means, in terms of the difficulties of providing narratives, in terms of bodily reactions, and in the silences and gaps that punctuate the conversation. The proximity of such testimony to psychoanalysis is self-evident. Thus, although the public commemoration of survivors tends towards kitsch, reducing complex individuals to heroic role models in tragic settings, there is at the same time a scholarship that informs museum practice and other forms of public history to the effect that what Henry Greenspan calls "the romancing of survival" is not appropriate. Greenspan cites one survivor, Sally Grubman, who in an interview in the late 1970s was already commenting on this phenomenon:

> We are not heroes. We survived by some fluke that we do not ourselves understand. And people have said, "Sally, tell the children about the joy of survival." And I can see that they don't understand it at all. If you're in a canoe and your life is in danger for a few minutes and you survive, you can talk about the joy of survival. We went through fire and ashes and whole families were destroyed. And we are left. How can we talk about the joy of survival?[31]

The growth of trauma theory—in parallel in literary scholarship and psychoanalysis—is but the most notable of the developments in psychoanalytical theory in recent decades. Where the question of the relationship between survival and the Holocaust is concerned, many other psychoanalytical concepts and ideas have been called into question and modified. Perhaps most important among these is the idea of identification with the aggressor. Bruno Bettelheim, in particular, borrowed this concept from Anna Freud and Sándor Ferenczi, and argued that camp inmates regressed to a childlike state in which identifying with their aggressors—the guards— was a form of infantile defense mechanism. In an important article on Bettelheim, Christian Fleck and Albert Müller cite Ernst Federn, who was in Buchenwald with Bettelheim and whom we will encounter again in Chap. 4:

> Bettelheim and I had noticed the degree to which the mechanisms of defence that Sándor Ferenczi and Anna Freud have described as identifica-

---

[30] Pinchevski, "Counter-testimony, Counter-archive", 245.
[31] Cited in Greenspan, *On Listening to Holocaust Survivors*, 45.

tion with the aggressor could be observed amongst the camp inmates. Who made the first observation I cannot tell today, but it was a significant one. What Anna Freud had described of children and what every nursery-school teacher can confirm can also be found among adults and most clearly when they are in a regressed state of mind.[32]

Fleck and Müller then note that Anna Freud related identification with the aggressor primarily to children in 1936:

In "identification with the aggressor" we recognize a by no means uncommon stage in the normal development of the superego. When the two boys whose cases I have just described identified themselves with their elders' threats of punishment, they were taking an important step toward the formation of that institution: they were internalizing other people's criticisms of their behavior. When a child constantly repeats this process of internalization and introjects the qualities of those responsible for his upbringing, making their characteristics and opinions his own, he is all the time providing material from which the superego may take shape.[33]

We might add that Ferenczi had also developed this idea long before the war, in an article first published in 1922.[34] And although Fleck and Müller say that it is beyond the scope of their work to historicize psychoanalytic categories, they do note that Bettelheim's interpretation "makes no fundamental distinction between the worlds of those who are imprisoned and those not imprisoned, a distinction that appears justified in the light of observations by other authors."[35]

Very few scholars today would use the concept of "identification with the aggressor" as a way of describing the behavior of concentration camp

---

[32] Ernst Federn, *Witnessing Psychoanalysis: From Vienna back to Vienna* via *Buchenwald and the USA* (Abingdon: Routledge, 2018 [1990]), 5, cited in Christian Fleck and Albert Müller, "Bruno Bettelheim and the Concentration Camps", *Journal of the History of the Behavioral Sciences*, 33:1 (1997), 18.

[33] Anna Freud, *The Ego and the Mechanisms of Defense* (New York: International Universities Press, 1971), 116, cited in Fleck and Müller, "Bruno Bettelheim", 18. The relevant chapter from Freud's book is also published as Anna Freud, "Identification with the Aggressor (1936)", in *Selected Writings*, eds. Richard Ekins and Ruth Freeman (London: Penguin, 1998), 13–23.

[34] Sándor Ferenczi, "The Confusion of Tongues between the Adults and the Child (The Language of Tenderness and Passion)", *International Journal of Psycho-analysis*, 30 (1949 [1922]), 225–230.

[35] Fleck and Müller, "Bruno Bettelheim", 18–19.

inmates. Certainly, there is considerable discussion of the camps as "class" societies, in which hierarchies prevailed, ethnic and linguistic differences between inmates were heightened, and where privileges were fought for. Leo Eitinger referred to kapos and other "privileged prisoners" in this context.[36] But perhaps precisely this greater understanding of "everyday life" in the camps has diminished the explanatory power, in this context, of "identification with the aggressor": it is far too simplistic and general to account for a situation that was not akin to the relationship between adults and children. Fleck and Müller suggest that considering the camps as a problem of deviance from ordinary life, manifesting as a regression to a childlike state, as Bettelheim did, means failing to think of them in terms of "a problem of complex survival strategies in the specific camp universe."[37] As we will see, concepts such as "stupor," "estrangement," and "depersonalization" seem, in light of recent historiography, more compelling as ways of understanding how inmates behaved in the camps. For the time being, it perhaps suffices to cite Curt Bondy, whose article on Buchenwald was published in the same issue of the *Journal of Abnormal and Social Psychology* as Bettelheim's more famous piece on extreme situations:

What were the effects of this treatment upon the prisoners? No one will be astonished that many internees completely broke down physically, psychologically, and morally. Such treatment would cause similar reactions in any large group of human beings.

The urge of self-preservation, bestial fear, hunger, and thirst led to a complete transformation of the majority of the prisoners. Never before—not even during the last war—had I witnessed such a loss of self-control. The ruthless struggle of "each against all" began. No one spoke in ordinary tones, every one screamed. Some even satisfied their physical needs on the spot. The main thing was to get something to eat and to drink. When food was brought in, an excitement ensued which one can otherwise observe only among animals.[38]

---

[36] Leo Eitinger, "Auschwitz—A Psychological Perspective", in Yisrael Gutman and Michael Berenbaum (eds.), *Anatomy of the Auschwitz Death Camp* (Bloomington: Indiana University Press/Washington, DC: United States Holocaust Memorial Museum, 1994), 474. Eitinger goes on to say (474–475) that "identifying with the aggressor proved to be a negative coping mechanism which eventually led to the destruction of those prisoners or, in the few cases where they survived, to deep pathological personality changes."

[37] Fleck and Müller, "Bruno Bettelheim", 19.

[38] Curt Bondy, "Problems of Internment Camps", *Journal of Abnormal and Social Psychology*, 38:4 (1943), 455.

Among other psychoanalytic concepts that have emerged in response to the Holocaust but which have not stood the test of time, none is as contentious as "concentration camp syndrome" or "survivor syndrome." This term, coined by William Niederland in the early 1960s, suggested that Holocaust survivors were on the whole deeply damaged psychologically. Hamburger shows that recent research to some extent reiterates that finding, one large-scale study concluding that Holocaust survivors "were less well adjusted, particularly showing substantially more posttraumatic stress symptoms than the non-exposed groups," although, somewhat paradoxically, also that they "showed remarkable resilience."[39] Holocaust survivors also, according to other studies, display similar kinds of PTSD symptoms as survivors of the genocide in Rwanda and slave labourers, symptoms including:

> that survivors do not have a life history in the form of a coherent autobiographical narrative and that they display an erasure of feelings of sorts, comprising a massive denial and/or disavowal of trauma, extreme ambiguity, speechlessness, psychotic or seemingly psychotic delusions, and other psychosomatic symptoms, replacement of repressed or split-off memories by screen memories, frequent nightmares, flashback memories, as well as daydreams of persecution.[40]

Yet, although this list partly recapitulates W. G. Niederland's from 1961, few psychoanalysts would today use the term "concentration camp syndrome" or "survivor syndrome," as it imposes too simple and coherent

---

[39] Hamburger, "Genocidal Trauma", 76–77. See also the findings of Efrat Barel, Abraham Sagi-Schwartz, Marinus H. Van IJzendoorn, and Marian J. Bakermans-Kranenburg, "Surviving the Holocaust: A Meta-Analysis of the Long-Term Sequelae of a Genocide", *Psychological Bulletin*, 136:5 (2010), 677–698; Marianne Amir and Rachel Lev-Wiesel, "Time Does Not Heal All Wounds: Quality of Life and Psychological Distress of People Who Survived the Holocaust as Children 55 Years Later", *Journal of Traumatic Stress*, 16:3 (2003), 295–299; S. Robinson, M. Rapaport-Bar-Sever, and J. Rapaport, "The Present State of People Who Survived the Holocaust as Children", *Acta Psychiatrica Scandinavica*, 89:4 (1999), 242–245.

[40] Hamburger, "Genocidal Trauma", 78–79, summarising the findings of Dori Laub, "Traumatic Shutdown of Narrative and Symbolization", in Laub and Hamburger (eds.), *Psychoanalysis and Holocaust Testimony*, 43–65.

a label on to a complex and multifaceted problem.[41] Indeed, Avi Kay notes that earlier studies that led to the coining of the term lacked methodological rigor, were based on small samples, relied too heavily on the presuppositions of the health professionals involved, and, in an ironic twist, exaggerated the generalizability of their findings in an attempt to force the hand of the recalcitrant West German restitution assessors—a noble aim but one that hid the variability of psychological symptoms and the range of survivors' abilities to cope.[42] Today the problem, as mentioned above, is the opposite one of survivors being heroized and homogenized in a different but no less simplistic way.

Psychoanalysis is an interpretive, therapeutic practice involving two people in a private, intense exchange or, since Bion's experiments of the 1940s onwards, varieties of group therapy. The issue of transference and countertransference means that, as a perusal through the back issues of the major psychoanalytical journals shows, there is no certainty in psychoanalysis, and that concepts and practices are continually changing. This is a normal description of the functioning of science and art. But when it comes to the relevance of psychoanalysis for understanding the Holocaust and vice-versa, this ever-changing ground raises difficult questions. It is not hard to find contradictory positions being held by theorists of psychoanalysis: Holocaust survivors suffer disproportionately from psychosis, *or* Holocaust survivors are unusually resilient and well adjusted; when Holocaust survivors give testimony, especially video testimony, one witnesses the crisis of testimony and the failure of narrative, *or* giving testimony is a therapeutic act for Holocaust survivors; the Holocaust provides a model for understanding trauma as such, *or* the Holocaust exceeds what is understood by trauma in the DSM and this excess manifests in survivors' symptoms. These debates offer a challenging yet rewarding way into

---

[41] See Niederland, "The Problem of the Survivor"; Niederland, "Clinical Observations on the 'Survivor Syndrome'", *International Journal of Psycho-analysis*, 49 (1968), 313–315. The concept of "survivor guilt", however, remains in currency and can still be productive; see, for example, John J. Hartman, "Anna Freud and the Holocaust: Mourning and Survivor Guilt", *International Journal of Psycho-analysis*, 95:6 (2014), 1183–1210, and Ruth Jaffe's earlier, powerful article, "The Sense of Guilt within Holocaust Survivors", *Jewish Social Studies*, 32:4 (1970), 307–314.

[42] Avi Kay, "The Impact of Attitudes toward the Holocaust and Holocaust Survivors in the United States, on the Adult Psychological Development of American Holocaust Survivors", in Johannes-Dieter Steinert and Inge Weber-Newth (eds.), *Beyond Camps and Forced Labour: Current International Research on Survivors of Nazi Persecution* (Osnabrück: Secolo, 2005), 600–602.

addressing some of the major issues surrounding Holocaust survival. And many of these interpretive disputes find echoes in the historiography of the Holocaust.

* * *

In one of the first postwar books on the Holocaust, Stefan Szende wrote about the ghetto in Lvov:

> Those few children who were left in the ghetto were ordinary children like any others. They cried bitterly when they were hungry and they clamored for bread. There were frightened and they trembled when the S.S. came, and their favorite game was pretending to carry out an "action."
> During the day they used to play in the yards and on the streets. We could often see them. One group would be the S.S. Another group the Ukrainian militia. A third group the Jewish police, and the majority would be the hunted Jews. They did not stop playing this terrible game even when S.S. and Ukrainian militiamen were marching through the streets. We sometimes saw the S.S. stop and watch the children playing this "action" game of theirs. And on one occasion I saw an S.S. man go to the children and give them advice as to how to play it properly.
> In their homes the children sang the songs of the S.S. they played at marching around in formation like the S.S., and singing the tune and even the text of notorious German songs.
> The life led by the women who had to stay at home in the crowded houses—there were no Jewish men at home by that time, except those in hiding—was hell on earth. With the best will in the world and the determination to help each other as far as possible in their difficulties, it was impossible to keep the rooms clean and tidy, or be as tolerant and cheerful as they would have liked.[43]

Theodor Adorno noted in *Negative Dialectics* that after Auschwitz, fearing death means fearing something worse than death.[44] A psychoanalytic study of survival of the Nazi camps backs up Freud's insight written in the aftermath of the Great War, which makes the same point as Adorno but, so to speak, from the opposite angle: "We have no longer to reckon

---

[43] Stefan Szende, *The Promise Hitler Kept*, trans. Edward Fitzgerald (London: Victor Gollancz, 1945), 238.

[44] Theodor W. Adorno, *Negative Dialectics*, trans. E. B. Ashton (London: Routledge, 1990), 371.

with the organism's puzzling determination (so hard to fit into any context) to maintain its own existence in the face of every obstacle. What we are left with is the fact that the organism wishes to die only in its own fashion."[45]

---

[45] Sigmund Freud, "Beyond the Pleasure Principle" (1920), in Angela Richards (ed.), *The Penguin Freud Library, Volume II: On Metapsychology. The Theory of Psychoanalysis* (London: Penguin, 1991), 311–312.

CHAPTER 2

Survival Through Stupor: Eddy de Wind and Early-Postwar Psychoanalytic Studies of the Nazi Concentration Camps

Abstract Eddy de Wind's *Last Stop Auschwitz* was written in a few weeks while de Wind was working as a survivor-physician with Soviet medics in post-liberation Auschwitz. The book, as well as de Wind's subsequent prolific output in psychiatry journals, merit analysis not only because in his professional writing he adumbrated what later became known as PTSD and much of the underpinnings of trauma theory. He also advocated a theory of survival that offers a compelling contrast to well-known "self-help" theories put forward by Bruno Bettelheim and, especially, Viktor Frankl. This chapter traces the ways in which de Wind's theory of survival challenged the simplistic narratives that were already emerging about the Nazi crimes in the late 1940s, explains how his writing informed the changing field of psychiatry after the war, and considers the relevance of his work for the historiography of the Holocaust today. From the perspective of history of ideas, I argue that the reception and publication of de Wind's book then and now—including the kitsch marketing of the latest English version—tells a story about the ways in which "Holocaust consciousness" has changed over the decades, sometimes in problematic ways.

Keywords Auschwitz • Holocaust • Survival • Psychoanalysis • Trauma

© The Author(s), under exclusive license to Springer Nature Switzerland AG 2024
D. Stone, *Psychoanalysis, Historiography, and the Nazi Camps*, The Holocaust and its Contexts,
https://doi.org/10.1007/978-3-031-58010-9_2

According to the German psychotherapist Hilde O. Bluhm, writing in 1948, "Death in a Nazi concentration camp requires no explanation. Survival does."[1] In the years immediately following the war, many psychologists and psychoanalysts turned their attention to the Nazi camps, taking up Bluhm's claim. But there was nothing like consensus amongst them. Beginning with the well-known and still extraordinarily popular work of Viktor Frankl and Bruno Bettelheim, this chapter shows how psychoanalytic theories that provided more sober versions of survival were submerged under the weight of the "positive thinking" that proved so compatible with the zeitgeist of the 1950s and 1960s. Today, the theories of survival put forward by neglected analysts such as the Dutch survivors of Auschwitz Eddy de Wind (1916–1987), Louis Micheels (1917–2008), and Elie A. Cohen (1909–1993), appear to be much more in keeping with the ways in which our understanding of the Holocaust has changed in light of several decades' worth of intensive, detailed, and methodologically innovative and varied historiography. I begin by analyzing the arguments of these three Dutch inmate-physicians who survived Auschwitz and went on to practice as psychoanalysts, drawing on their memoirs and from their analytical and clinical writings. There is little evidence in the texts that the three men discussed here were close, but a few references to de Wind and Cohen in Micheels' memoir indicates that they certainly knew each other. Cohen and de Wind arrived at Auschwitz on the same transport from Westerbork, for example, and both stepped forward when doctors were ordered to do so.[2] I then argue that the incipient theory of trauma that they (among other analysts such as Hans Keilson) were developing had little purchase in the postwar period, for reasons internal to psychoanalysis and because of wider cultural presuppositions. Today, by contrast, their work makes sense, psychoanalytically and historiographically speaking, in ways that it could not in earlier decades.

Two years before Bluhm's article appeared, Viktor Frankl claimed that the "apparent paradox that some prisoners of a less hardy make-up seemed to survive camp life better than did those of a robust nature" could be explained by virtue of the fact that such "sensitive people … were able to

---

[1] Hilde O. Bluhm, "How Did They Survive? Mechanisms of Defense in Nazi Concentration Camps", *American Journal of Psychotherapy*, 53:1 (1999), 96–122 (96). See Chap. 4 for more detail.

[2] Louis J. Micheels, *Doctor #117641: A Holocaust Memoir* (New Haven: Yale University Press, 1989), 117, where Micheels refers to Ed and Elie among other Dutch inmates. Elie A. Cohen, *The Abyss: A Confession*, trans. James Brockway (New York: W. W. Norton & Company, 1973), 83, on Cohen's and de Wind's arrival at Auschwitz.

retreat from their terrible surroundings to a life of inner riches and spiritual freedom."[3] Similarly, although from a different therapeutic perspective, Bruno Bettelheim argued that even if luck was the first prerequisite for survival, "most of all ... autonomy, self-respect, inner integration, a rich inner life, and the ability to relate to others in meaningful ways were the psychological conditions which, more than any others, permitted one to survive in the camps as much a whole human being as overall conditions and chance would permit."[4]

Critics have pointed out that Frankl's claims not only served to ingratiate him with the Austrian authorities—by deflecting attention from the perpetrators to the victims—but marginalized those victims who died by implying that they lacked the right will to live. Lawrence Langer, writing over 40 years ago, was one of the first to call Frankl's credentials into question, arguing that "intoxicated by his therapeutic view of human experience, including the Holocaust, Frankl makes physical survival a matter of mental health."[5] There were no doubt some survivors who believed that their survival was due to those factors proposed by Frankl, that is, a conscious desire to want to live. Margareta Glas-Larsson is one such who attributes her survival to an unfailingly positive attitude.[6] But the critics are unpersuaded that this constitutes a convincing explanation for Hilde Bluhm's problem.

Similar criticisms have been levelled against Bettelheim, from claims that he lied about his qualifications to charges of plagiarism, to those who object to his claim that inmates identified with the guards and (most

[3] Viktor Frankl, *From Death-Camp to Existentialism: A Psychiatrist's Path to a New Therapy* (Boston: Beacon Press, 1961 [orig. 1946]), 35, cited in Timothy Pytell, "Viktor Frankl's Flight into the Spiritual", in Zeev Mankowitz, David Weinberg and Sharon Kangisser Cohen (eds.), *Europe in the Eyes of Survivors of the Holocaust* (Jerusalem: Yad Vashem, 2014), 138. *From Death-Camp to Existentialism* was subsequently republished as *Man's Search for Meaning*.

[4] Bruno Bettelheim, "Owners of Their Faces", in Bettelheim, *Surviving the Holocaust* (London: Fontana, 1986), 101.

[5] Lawrence L. Langer, *Versions of Survival: The Holocaust and the Human Spirit* (Albany, NY: State University of New York Press, 1982), 26. The criticisms have been most substantially developed by Timothy Pytell; see: "Viktor Frankl's Flight"; "The Missing Pieces of the Puzzle: A Reflection on the Odd Career of Viktor Frankl", *Journal of Contemporary History*, 35:2 (2000), 281–306; "Redeeming the Unredeemable: Auschwitz and *Man's Search for Meaning*", *Holocaust and Genocide Studies*, 17:1 (2003), 89–113; "Extreme Experience, Psychological Insight, and Holocaust Perception: Reflections on Bettelheim and Frankl", *Psychoanalytic Psychology*, 24:4 (2007), 641–657; *Viktor Frankl's Search for Meaning: An Emblematic 20th-Century Life* (New York: Berghahn Books, 2015).

[6] Margareta Glas-Larsson, *I Want to Live: The Tragedy and Banality of Survival in Terezin and Auschwitz*, ed. Gerhard Botz (Riverside, CA: Ariadne, 1991).

relevant here), assertions that his theories of survival led ultimately to blaming the victims—most famously in his essay on Anne Frank and her family where he argued that they failed to survive by not hiding well enough and not having a gun.[7] Robert Krell accused Bettelheim of maligning survivors.[8] It is not necessary to rehearse these well-known arguments here.[9] It is, nevertheless, worth pointing out that Ernst Federn, the son of the noted Freudian psychoanalyst Paul Federn, who knew Bettelheim in Dachau and Buchenwald, observed that by the time Bettelheim was in the latter camp (September 1938–April 1939), it had become a "work camp" where "life was very bad indeed, but it was possible to survive, even for a person as unsuited to the practicalities of life as Bettelheim." Federn then noted of Bettelheim that "He owed his survival to the chance of finding work in the stock-mending shop, where he could live in relative safely," thus discreetly passing over Bettelheim's supposedly psychoanalytically informed theories without comment.[10] Another psychologist who mistrusted Bettelheim's claims in *The Informed Heart* was the Dutch survivor Eddy de Wind, who noted calmly that he had "quite a few

---

[7] Bettelheim, "The Ignored Lesson of Anne Frank", in *Surviving the Holocaust*, 120–132. Bettelheim then claimed (124) that he was not criticizing what the Frank family did—"A family has every right to arrange their life as they wish or think best, and to take the risks they want to take"—but "only the universal admiration of their way of coping, or rather of not coping."

[8] Robert Krell, "Psychiatry and the Holocaust", in Robert Krell and Marc I. Sherman, *Medical and Psychological Effects of Concentration Camps on Holocaust Survivors* (New Brunswick: Transaction Publishers, 1997), 5–6.

[9] For a critical appraisal, see Paul Roazen, "The Rise and Fall of Bruno Bettelheim", *The Psychohistory Review*, 20:3 (1992), 221–250, and, especially, Nathalie Zajde, "The Holocaust and the Limits of Psychoanalysis: The Case of Bruno Bettelheim", in Jean-Marc Dreyfus and Daniel Langton (eds.), *Writing the Holocaust* (London: Bloomsbury Academic, 2011), 116–135, who calls Bettelheim's argument "quite simply wrong" (129). For critical but more cautiously sympathetic analyses, see Paul Marcus and Alan Rosenberg, "Reevaluating Bruno Bettelheim's Work on the Nazi Concentration Camps", *The Psychoanalytic Review*, 81:3 (1994), 537–563, and Christian Fleck and Albert Müller, "Bruno Bettelheim and the Concentration Camps", *Journal of the History of the Behavioral Sciences*, 33:1 (1997), 1–37. See also the useful discussion in Kim Wünschmann, "The 'Scientification' of the Concentration Camp: Early Theories of Terror and Their Reception by American Academia", *Leo Baeck Institute Yearbook*, 58 (2013), 111–126.

[10] Ernst Federn, *Witnessing Psychoanalysis: From Vienna back to Vienna via Buchenwald and the USA* (Abingdon: Routledge, 2018 [1990]), 4. Federn did, however, go on to talk of Bettelheim in complimentary terms. On Federn's experiences in Buchenwald, see also his 1956 account for the Wiener Library (P.III.h. No. 228. Buchenwald), online at: https://www.testifyingtothetruth.co.uk/viewer/image/105742/1/

objections" to the book.[11] Not least was the fact that Bettelheim had not been in an extermination camp and did not appreciate the conditions faced by the inmates in a place such as Auschwitz. He added that sustaining life in a concentration camp was more of an "art" than the result of "intelligent adaptation," as Bettelheim claimed.[12] Like many later critics of Bettelheim, from Terrence Des Pres onwards, de Wind objected to the absence of consideration of the social factors that shaped the inmates' lives; in other words, the fact of being in a concentration camp, with all that implies—not least the need for mutual support from other inmates[13]— was missing from Bettelheim's psychological explanation of survival.

Before turning to de Wind, first we must note, as did Elie Cohen in *Human Behaviour in the Concentration Camp*, that "many newcomers were not given the chance of adaptation: either because, as in the extermination camps they were gassed immediately upon arrival, or because they simply collapsed under the hard work and the abominable circumstances."[14] Besides, there were also long-term camp inmates who did not have a similar hope; indeed, some of them "seemed totally to have given up hope in a concrete realistic future, lost their autonomy, and may have identified with the values of the SS."[15] Nevertheless, as studies of survivors have shown, many have "positive coping skills" and "an unusual ability to adjust and obtain a new internal integration."[16] This is not the same as

[11] Eddy de Wind, *Confrontatië met de dood: Psychische gevolgen van vervolging* (Utrecht: ICODO, 1993), 27 ("Ik heb echter nogal wat bezwaren tegen dit boek en de daarin beschreven psychodynamieken").

[12] de Wind, *Confrontatië met de dood*, 32 ("Ik zou hieraan toe willen voegen dat het in een bepaald opzicht meer een kunst was als men het leven in een concentratiekamp volhield, dan het resultaat van intelligente anpassing").

[13] A criticism made by Elmer Luchterhand, "Prisoner Behavior and Social System in the Nazi Concentration Camps", *International Journal of Social Psychology*, 13 (1964), 245–264. For a measured defence of Bettelheim, see Paul Marcus, *Autonomy in the Extreme Situation: Bruno Bettelheim, the Nazi Concentration Camps, and the Mass Society* (Westport, CT: Praeger, 1999).

[14] Elie A. Cohen, *Human Behaviour in the Concentration Camp*, trans. M. H. Braaksma (London: Free Association Books, 1988 [1952]), 147–148.

[15] Amy Louise Adamczyk, "Frankl, Bettelheim and the Camps", *Journal of Genocide Research*, 7:1 (2005), 81.

[16] Jacob Lomranz, "The Skewed Image of the Holocaust Survivor and the Vicissitudes of Holocaust Research", *Echoes of the Holocaust: Bulletin of the Jerusalem Center for Research into the Late Effects of the Holocaust*, 6 (2000), 48. See also Robert Krell, "Resilience", in Ira Brenner (ed.), *The Handbook of Psychoanalytic Holocaust Studies: International Perspectives* (London: Routledge, 2020), 41–51, and, especially, the work of John Sigal: Cécile Rousseau, "Diving into Complexity: John Sigal's Work on the Long-Term Consequences of the Holocaust", *Clinical Child Psychology and Psychiatry*, 10:2 (2005), 262–265.

saying that they survived because of those skills but that human beings who have survived traumatic events can lead reasonably well-adjusted lives. Rather than suggest that all survivors suffered from William Niederland's famous "survivor syndrome"—a "pathological category" that, as Emily Kuriloff notes, following survivor analyst Anna Ornstein, did a great deal of damage to survivors[17]—or were all heroically unaffected by their persecution, I want to suggest that a more nuanced approach is desirable. This requires some attention to the history of psychoanalysis, especially that discipline's supposed failure to grapple with the Holocaust (I say "supposed" because despite the impressive evidence brought forward by Kuriloff, Hans Reijzer, and others, in fact psychoanalysts and psychologists were among the first to address the Nazi camps during and after the war). It also requires paying attention to insights from psychoanalysis and psychotherapy that pertain to the perpetrators—especially the appeal of Nazism—and, of particular relevance to this chapter, the victims.[18] That includes of course some psychoanalysts, whose own histories need to be understood as intimately connected, though not in a determinist fashion, to their professional work. This chapter considers why a theory of survival quite different from Frankl's and Bettelheim's, though penned at the same time, has had little purchase or resonance until recently. I suggest that only after decades of historical research into the Nazi camp system, consideration of postwar testimonies, and struggles within and involving the psychoanalytic community—especially over restitution claims—have historians and psychoanalysts been able to grasp in a sober fashion the true heinousness of the Nazi crimes, meaning that wishful thinking about the "human spirit" and the like no longer appears convincing.

Until 2020, Eddy de Wind's *Eindstation Auschwitz* was known only to Dutch speakers. The book, written in a few weeks while de Wind was working as a survivor-physician with Soviet medics in post-liberation Auschwitz, and reckoned to be the only book completed in Auschwitz while the camp was still in existence, was published in Dutch by the

[17] Emily A. Kuriloff, *Contemporary Psychoanalysis and the Legacy of the Third Reich: History, Memory, Tradition* (New York: Routledge, 2014), 31.

[18] Following Roger Frie, *Not in My Family: German Memory and Responsibility after the Holocaust* (New York: Oxford University Press, 2017), 241–242 n4, I use the terms "psychoanalysis" and "psychotherapy" interchangeably, since the historical separation between them no longer holds. The relevance of psychoanalysis for understanding the Nazi perpetrators is beyond the scope of this chapter, but see the introduction above for brief comments.

communist publishing house De Republiek de Letteren in 1946. Reissued only once in Dutch (by Van Gennep in 1980), although an excerpt also appeared in Adler, Langbein, and Lingens-Reiner's well-known *Auschwitz: Zeugnisse und Berichte*,[19] it has recently appeared in English as *Last Stop Auschwitz* and numerous other translations. The book, as well as de Wind's subsequent output in psychiatry journals, merit consideration not only because in his professional writing he adumbrated what later became known as PTSD and much of the underpinnings of trauma theory. He also advocated a theory of survival that offers a compelling contrast to well-known "self-help" theories put forward by Bettelheim and, especially, Frankl. As we will see, like other Dutch survivor-physicians, such as Louis Micheels and Elie Cohen, de Wind proposed a more sober analysis of survival, in his case centered on the concept of "stupor."

In *Last Stop Auschwitz*, de Wind's protagonist is named Hans van Dam, though it is clear that in every detail the book is autobiographical. Although it omits the first stages of de Wind's actual camp journey, from volunteering to work as an inmate doctor at Westerbork in 1942 in order to help his mother, to meeting and marrying his wife Friedel in Westerbork, the story of Hans, most of which covers his time in Block 9 at Auschwitz I, is obviously about de Wind himself. Hans works first at Block 28 and is lucky to have several meetings with his wife, also called Friedel, who is in Block 10. She also sends him food when she can. After two weeks, Hans is transferred to Block 9, where he works as assistant to the admissions doctor. After a few weeks, Hans understands—at least in retrospect—what Auschwitz means:

> Auschwitz was more than torment writ large. With its factories and mines it was an important part of the Upper Silesian industrial area and its workers were cheaper than anywhere else in the world. They didn't need pay and they ate almost nothing. And then, when they were exhausted and fell victim to the gas chamber, there were still enough Jews and political opponents in Europe to make up the numbers yet again.[20]

---

[19] Eduard de Wind, "Der Experimentierblock," in H. G. Adler, Hermann Langbein and Ella Lingens-Reiner (eds.), *Auschwitz: Zeugnisse und Berichte*, 6th edn (Bonn: Bundeszentrale für politische Bildung, 2014), 175–178.
[20] Eddy de Wind, *Last Stop Auschwitz: My Story of Survival from within the Camp*, trans. David Colmer (London: Black Swan, 2020), 81.

Witnessing numerous deadly beatings, being transferred to the quarantine block and a stint in the *Strafkommando* (punishment squad), and finding ways of remaining in touch with Friedel, Hans adapts to life in the camp, aware of the fortune his position brings him—as well as the risks. He survives several moves, ending up as a *Pfleger* (nurse) in Block 19, where he is able to remain when the camp is evacuated in January 1945. The story itself is not my focus here, although given when it was written, de Wind's narrative is remarkably trenchant and level-headed. Rather, here I want to focus on how de Wind reflected on his experiences after the evacuation of the camp and later on, when trying to explain his survival. At the end of the book, Hans ponders his survival, asking himself: "Why was he alive? What gave him the right to live? In what way was he better than all those millions who had died?"[21] It fell to de Wind, rather than his alter ego Hans, to address those questions in the years after Auschwitz.

In "Confrontation with Death," first published in 1949, de Wind argues that in order to survive the concentration camp, the inmate had neither to "surrender completely" nor to "resist with all his vitality"—both were sure paths to death. Rather, he proposed "the paradox that reconciling oneself to death was a vital condition for the prisoner" and that what he called the "death principle" (which he named so as to be distinguishable from Freud's "death drive"), which in ordinary life should be kept at bay, was "a necessity" in the camp. The inmate, in other words, had to develop a "camp psyche," a state of stupor that did not completely dominate but was characterized by a "a form of inner acceptance" of death, tempered by the preservation of just enough vitality "to give the right answer at critical moments." He provides an example of a patient who, as de Wind said, "found the right style" and developed—not consciously—"a remarkable capacity to let insult and injury pass him by virtually unnoticed."[22] This was not a man who devoted himself to religious or political ideas or sought out the solace and support of comradeship but a man who himself did not understand how he had survived. If readers did not want to hear such analysis, it was not only because of the changed political circumstances of emerging Cold War Europe but because, as de Wind pointed out, even "years after the war" (he was writing in 1949!), "we regularly see how difficult it is to reverse the far-reaching alteration of personality that took place in the camps." After "Confrontation with

---

[21] de Wind, *Last Stop Auschwitz*, 206.
[22] de Wind, "Confrontation with Death", in *Last Stop Auschwitz*, 250–251.

Death," de Wind furthered his argument with case studies that he examined in later articles.

By the time these articles were published in the 1970s and 1980s, de Wind's arguments were starting to make sense in the psychoanalytic community and beyond, thanks to the "discovery" of PTSD in the wake of the Vietnam War.[23] Although the clinical understanding of "trauma" is often attributed to an attempt to make sense of the symptoms displayed by American veterans of Vietnam (with the exception of the scandal of My Lai, the focus was almost never on their victims), in fact we can now see that psychoanalysts were groping towards an understanding of similar symptoms that had been exhibited by Holocaust survivors since the end of the war. The question here is not the novelty of the symptoms but why the prevailing attitude towards them changed sufficiently for clinicians to be able to "see" them in a way that had previously not been possible. As de Wind noted in an article from 1984: "Immediately after the war General Practitioners as well as most psychiatrists thought that only a few of the victims of the Nazis would suffer from their dreadful experiences for a long time or perhaps for the rest of their lives. Psychoanalysts," he then went on, "could have known better."[24] Referring to the post-Great War focus on "war neurosis" as well as the recognition after World War II of the possibility of "lasting effects of concentration camp traumatization," de Wind implies that at that point, the idea put forward by his Dutch colleague Jacques Tas that "the traumatization was so massive that an irreversible injury would occur" was not yet one that psychoanalysis was ready to accept.[25] Nevertheless, 13 years earlier, in an article of 1971, de Wind had himself been less decisive, arguing cautiously that "traumatization by persecution (or other traumatic events in adult life) is probably always unconsciously linked with memories of infantile traumata," and "The problem of psychic trauma in adult life seems to be in contradiction to the psychoanalytic theories of the importance of the early life in determining

---

[23] For example: "Persecution, Aggression and Therapy", *International Journal of Psychoanalysis*, 53:2 (1972), 173–177.

[24] E. de Wind, "Some Implications of Former Massive Traumatization upon the Actual Analytic Process", *International Journal of Psycho-analysis*, 65:3 (1984), 273.

[25] de Wind, "Some Implications", 273. See also Ferenc Erős, "From War Neurosis to Holocaust Trauma: An Intellectual and Cultural History", *SIMON. Shoah: Intervention, Methods, Documentation*, 4:1 (2017), 41–58, for discussion.

the personality patterns as well as the nature of the emotional problems."[26] He acquired more confidence in his views over time, as his clinical practice developed.

De Wind's use of the term "traumatization" in the 1970s and 1980s followed Henry Krystal's ground-breaking study of 1968, *Massive Psychic Trauma*, as well as works by Robert Lifton and "so many publications on Vietnam victims, etc. (unfortunately)."[27] In *Massive Psychic Trauma*, Krystal and Niederland argued, on the basis of 20 years of clinical practice with camp survivors, that "we are dealing here with victims of a traumatization of such magnitude, severity, and duration as to produce a recognizable clinical syndrome."[28] This is not simply an aside; Krystal and Niederland's identification and definition of the "survivor syndrome" was connected to theories of survival. De Wind not only foreshadowed the concept of PTSD; he also put forward a proposition about which psychological predispositions facilitated survival. Krystal and Niederland took this idea further, arguing that the prevalence of psychosomatic illnesses among Holocaust survivors was revealing. "Whereas," they write, "people with schizophrenic or self-destructive tendencies were very quickly killed in the ghettos and concentration camps, selectively, the hyperalert and exceedingly pliable and adjustable individuals apparently had a better chance of survival."[29] This claim is not, I think, incompatible with de Wind's notion of "survival through stupor," for despite the emphasis on "stupor," this is a theory of adaptability. The occurrence of psychosomatic illnesses among survivors, then, especially in the group aged between 15 and 30 during the persecution, relates, according to Krystal and Niederland, to "the experience of overwhelming rage and despair under complete passivity." Whereas somatic symptoms occur less frequently in survivors who had been able to be active in their survival or who had fought the Nazis, for those who had to adapt and suppress their instincts in the way described by de Wind, the results are different: "Apparently,

---

[26] Eddy de Wind, "Psychotherapy after Traumatization Caused by Persecution", *International Psychiatry Clinics*, 8:1 (1971), 103 and 93.

[27] de Wind, "Some Implications", 273.

[28] H. Krystal and W. G. Niederland, "Clinical Observations on the Survivor Syndrome", in Henry Krystal (ed.), *Massive Psychic Trauma* (New York: International Universities Press, 1968), 327.

[29] Krystal and Niederland, "Clinical Observations on the Survivor Syndrome", 336.

passivity and especially arrest in motility, as in long periods of hiding in limited space, led to greater somatization of anxiety and tension."[30]

Arguments such as Krystal's were not without problems of their own. In somewhat cryptic language, Laurence Kahn writes that the concept of "extreme traumatic experience" contributed to "the rise of the notion of 'massive trauma', associated with a simplification of the concept of splitting, thereby fuelling the model of a psychic functioning mainly ruled by survival."[31] But this tendency to portray survivors in a uniform fashion, in the way suggested by "survivor syndrome," was nevertheless an advance on the previous attitude dominating the psychoanalytic profession, which was that trauma in adult life was caused in infancy and that social or group phenomena were of marginal concern (even recognizing that Freud was by no means dirigiste in this matter, as his later works on metapsychology, religion, and civilization show). This difficulty stemmed from the psychoanalytic profession's struggle to focus on anything other than the individual's unconscious and to accept that outside events could generate trauma in later life, even though Freud had provided the tools for grappling with such issues. As Werner Bohleber remarks, "The field of psychoanalysis was the inner world of the human being—the unconscious, and unconscious phantasies. For many analysts, the adequate integration of external reality seemed like an intrusion on psychic reality and the meaning of the unconscious."[32] Besides, survival was precisely what was at stake, if not survival in later life—although questions of resilience, suicide, and the struggle to find life worth living were themes that analysts grappled with in their clinical encounters with survivors—then at least with respect to the question of how the Nazis' victims survived the period of persecution.

[30] Krystal and Niederland, "Clinical Observations on the Survivor Syndrome", 337.
[31] Laurence Kahn, *What Nazism did to Psychoanalysis*, trans. Andrew Weller (London: Routledge, 2023), 5.
[32] Werner Bohleber, "Treatment, Trauma, and Catastrophic Reality: A Double Understanding of the 'Too Much' Experience and Its Implications for Treatment", in Dori Laub and Andreas Hamburger (eds.), *Psychoanalysis and Holocaust Testimony: Unwanted Memories of Social Trauma* (London: Routledge, 2017), 20. See also Lewis A. Kirshner, "Trauma and Psychosis: A Review and Framework for Psychoanalytic Understanding", *International Forum of Psychoanalysis* (2013), 1–9; and Kirshner, "Trauma, the Good Object, and the Symbolic: A Theoretical Integration", *International Journal of Psycho-Analysis*, 75:2 (1994), 235–242, where Kirshner seeks to find common ground between Ferenczi, Freud, Klein and Lacan in the notion of the "good object", i.e., the "symbolic representation of the human world of cultural meanings and value."

Thus, by the time that he published his later clinical articles, de Wind was making the case for the idea of "trauma" being caused by his patients' experiences under Nazi rule, thereby taking on the West German restitution process, which, in its insistence that survivors' illnesses were related to pre-existing childhood traumas, relied on an older psychoanalytic orthodoxy. But the analyses themselves remained consistent with his first postwar treatments. In 1971, he claimed that "the ability to regress had great survival value."[33] A year later, he repeated the claim: "The capacity to regress proved essential to survival."[34] These claims were made on the basis of clinical work with survivors. And by 1984, he was asserting that:

> Only those in whom the prerequisites for any form of quick adaptation existed, especially for a quick inversion of their view on life and death, had a chance to overcome the most difficult first weeks and months. … In normal life it is pathological if one can only think in terms of disaster and death. In the camp the paradox was that only those who were able to accept the certainty of having to die, could live on for the time being.[35]

This article from 1984 is especially noteworthy in that de Wind raised here, decades before analysts such as Kuriloff discussed it, the question of transference when dealing with patients traumatized by their camp experiences. He asked the question whether it might be better for traumatized patients to be treated by traumatized therapists, so that a more "'neutral' working-alliance could develop." He observed the reluctance of survivor or émigré analysts to treat Holocaust survivors, referring to a "conspiracy of silence" in the 1950s, citing one who said that "such horrible things were beyond the possibilities of analysis." And he concluded by noting that "The therapist has to have a special interest in the topic, in the social as well as in the psychodynamic aspects of the traumatization, but he should not be overruled by this interest, either in his private life or in his professional sphere."[36] It is hard to see how a therapist traumatized by the same events as his or her patient could provide a neutral therapeutic space. But this is an aside—the main point is that de Wind not only foreshadowed the acceptance of trauma as a genuine diagnosis but consistently

---

[33] de Wind, "Psychotherapy after Traumatization Caused by Persecution", 106.
[34] de Wind, "Persecution, Aggression and Therapy", 173.
[35] de Wind, "Some Implications", 273.
[36] de Wind, "Some Implications", 275.

offered, on the basis of his clinical and personal experience, a theory of survival that differed markedly from those prevailing in the postwar years. De Wind's arguments do not mark a complete break with those of Bettelheim or Frankl. On the role of spiritual life, for example, he writes: "In general in the camp we saw that those whose lives had some kind of religious alignment (this in the broadest sense, also as a devotion to a political system or a humanistic philosophy), were the quickest to recover from the initial stupor."[37] More important, de Wind's claims about the need to survive through stupor do not often seem to match the account given in *Last Stop Auschwitz*. The latter suggests a man very much working to sustain himself intellectually and spiritually, desperately maintaining his relationship with his wife in Block 10 and with other inmates, especially the Dutch men. Indeed, his descriptions of those relationships adds force to Anna Ornstein's argument that the creation of small groups was a crucial aid to survival in the camps.[38] Hans is certainly not in control of his own destiny but his manoeuvring suggests more than someone simply responding with the "right" answer when addressed by the guards; rather, he is a man seeking to adapt to the situation with guile and intelligence. Here we perhaps see an example of Kuriloff's argument that after the war psychoanalysts divorced their personal experience from their theories and clinical practice—albeit with a caveat in de Wind's case that, as we have seen, he by no means shied away from talking about and working with the victims of Nazi persecution. With de Wind, we see rather a tension between what he wrote in his transparently autobiographical account of Auschwitz and his later descriptions of working with survivors in a clinical setting, where he devised his theory of "stupor." Unlike Frankl, however, it is clear from his clinical practice that de Wind was not satisfied only with reference to the inmate's spiritual life. And neither was Elie Cohen, to whom we turn next.

Cohen cited de Wind's "Confrontation with Death" (the passage cited above about spiritual life) in his 1952 doctoral thesis, subsequently

---

[37] de Wind, "Confrontation with Death", 256–257.
[38] Anna Ornstein, "Mass Murder and the Individual: Psychoanalytic Reflections on Perpetrators and Their Victims", *International Journal of Group Psychotherapy*, 62:1 (2012), esp. 14–16. See also Norman R. Jackman, "Survival in the Concentration Camp", *Human Organization*, 17:2 (1958), 23–26, e.g. 26: "If the individual was unwilling or unable to belong to any membership group in camp, then his chances of physical survival were minimized."

published as *Human Behavior in the Concentration Camp*.[39] Cohen's long chapter on "the psychology of the concentration-camp prisoner" indicates three stages through which inmates passed: initial reaction, adaptation, and resignation. He is clear that "a prisoner's spiritual life was of very great importance, that it fitted him better for adaptation, and that through it he might considerably add to his chances of survival."[40] Yet, as we have already noted, Cohen criticized Bettelheim and Frankl for stopping there and for suggesting that inmates failed to help themselves; indeed, having stressed the importance of spiritual life, he then emphasized the need for inmates to *lower* their own spiritual standard, "since, if one wanted to survive, one could not but accept the standards prevailing in the camp."[41] As with de Wind, Cohen's scholarly work is not always in accord with his account of his own experiences, yet they seem more closely integrated than de Wind's. Cohen has much to say about depersonalization, regression, jealousy, group libido, and identification with the guards, but he always returns to "one factor that was entirely outside the prisoner's control: luck, fate, accident—call it what you like—which often caused the prisoner's life to take an unexpected turn."[42] The importance of a spiritual life, of resignation ("stupor"), and especially of luck are all apparent in Cohen's own account of survival.

Like de Wind, Elie Cohen was in Block 9 at Auschwitz, where he worked as a doctor, having previously held the same position at Westerbork. In his frank "confession," *The Abyss* (*De Afgrond: Een Egodocument*, 1971), based on a series of interviews that had appeared in the *Vrij Nederland*, Cohen says of himself that he "climbed the social ladder fairly quickly in Westerbork" and that based on his experiences he came to understand that "man is an egoist."[43] This is not explicitly the reason why his book is subtitled (in the Dutch edition) "an ego document" but it tells us a great deal about Cohen's understanding of his survival. He explains on several occasions that only his position as a doctor saved his life and that, ending as the case-reporting doctor in Block 9 "meant having an

---

[39] Cohen, *Human Behavior*, 148 (with a different translation).
[40] Cohen, *Human Behavior*, 150. Here one is reminded of arguments about Hasidic victims of the Holocaust, which often suggest that they "faced death with defiance" thanks to their faith. See, for example, Pesach Schindler, *Hasidic Responses to the Holocaust in the Light of Hasidic Thought* (Hoboken, NJ: Ktav Publishing House, 1990).
[41] Cohen, *Human Behavior*, 150.
[42] Cohen, *Human Behavior*, 179.
[43] Cohen, *The Abyss*, 59, 61.

important, prominent position."⁴⁴ He is unusually open about what his job meant: selecting others for transports, knowing that this meant delivering them to the gas chamber. "I don't want to say anything about other people," he writes, "for I haven't the right to. But I myself collaborated." This means that:

> I was honest (between inverted commas), as far as I could be. I was obedient and did the job I had to do in a completely, yes, "honest" way. That wasn't very nice of me; it wasn't decent, and it wasn't courageous. It is a fact, one of the facts, of which I am ashamed. I definitely wasn't extra mean, but—and this probably applies to everyone who came out of the concentration camps alive—I'm tarred. I allowed my own interests to prevail over the general good, or over an honest attitude in my life, based on principles.⁴⁵

Cohen then goes on to affirm Arendt's assessment of the Jewish Councils, including criticizing historian Jacques Presser for not being entirely frank about his own survival through his connections with the Joodse Raad, and in general shows that he in no way considers his survival to be a form of heroism.

In several important respects, however, his disarmingly frank "confession" somewhat mitigates his self-criticism. He insists on the overriding fact of being a doctor—and therefore prominent—but also notes the significance of having a close friend, Berthold Krebs, in Auschwitz; Cohen did not have his wife close by, as de Wind and Louis Micheels did, since she and their son had been murdered on arrival at Auschwitz. But above all, and here he comes close to confirming de Wind's theory of "stupor," he attributes his survival to looking to his own protection through what he calls "depersonalization": "You looked on, as though through a peephole, taking no part in things yourself. You watched. It didn't concern you."⁴⁶ Or as he wrote in his book *The Nineteen Trains to Sobibor*, "You had to learn to watch horrifying events with 'empty' eyes, you could not afford to feel pity, you had to get calluses on your soul, in brief, you had

---

⁴⁴ Cohen, *The Abyss*, 106. As he says elsewhere in the book (48): "I owe my life—absolutely, with no doubt whatever—to the fact that I'd studied medicine." See also *Human Behaviour*, 151.

⁴⁵ Cohen, *The Abyss*, 61. See also the 1988 preface to *Human Behaviour*, where he says the same thing but, with forty years hindsight, with explicit regret: "I should have drawn the line at my willingness to collaborate" (11).

⁴⁶ Cohen, *The Abyss*, 46.

to pass through a process of *customization*."⁴⁷ When he recounts a story of how close he came to death, Cohen affirms de Wind's theory that one needed a combination of acceptance of death and just enough vitality to give the right answer at crucial moments. When cleaning the windows in the ward, a high-ranking SS-man asked him what he was doing and he replied that he had been ordered to clean the windows:

> And then I could actually *see* that man thinking. I myself, of course, was standing stiffly at attention, and yes, I was looking at him. And I don't think I have ever been so close to death as at that moment. If I had batted an eyelid then, or had been wearing the wrong look—a smile—on my face, or had looked afraid or whatever, then one nod from him—no more, just one nod of his head—would have been enough. Apparently he didn't see anything so frightful in me, or anything unpleasant, or ... I don't know. I don't know how I acted. Anyway, he turned on his heels and off he went. Looking back, that was the most frightening moment I experienced there.⁴⁸

Thus, although he agrees with Frankl and de Wind that a spiritual life considerably added to the chances of survival, he goes further, adding that "the next condition essential for adaptation was *the lowering of one's own spiritual standard.*"⁴⁹ To this he adds, somewhat confusingly, the "drive for self-preservation," which sounds again like Frankl. But he concludes by citing Bluhm's 1948 study, which emphasized the "one great unpredictable force that ruled over life and death on the inmates. It was the *anarchic power of accident.*"⁵⁰ Cohen concurs, noting that the ability to adapt, which could take a year, was wholly dependent on the luck of surviving that long in the first place.⁵¹

What happened to Louis Micheels adds to the store of information backing up de Wind's and Cohen's arguments. Micheels, a medical student in Utrecht in 1940 when the Germans occupied The Netherlands, was captured with his fiancée Nora in October 1942 as the two of them

---

⁴⁷ Cohen, *De negentien treinen naar Sobibor* (1979), cited in Yehudi Lindeman, "Abandonment, Adjustment, and Memory: Reflections on J. Presser, Elie Cohen and Gerhard Durlacher", in Wolfgang Mieder and David Scrase (eds.), *Reflections on the Holocaust: Festschrift for Raul Hilberg on his Seventy-Fifth Birthday* (Burlington, VT: The Center for Holocaust Studies at the University of Vermont, 2001), 88.
⁴⁸ Cohen, *The Abyss*, 96.
⁴⁹ Cohen, *Human Behaviour*, 150 (emphasis in original).
⁵⁰ Cohen, *Human Behaviour*, 155, citing Bluhm, "How Did They Survive?", 20.
⁵¹ Cohen, *Human Behaviour*, 179.

were attempting to cross the border into Belgium. Held first in Mechelen (Malines), in April 1943 they were both deported to Auschwitz and separated. Micheels was initially sent to the slave labor plant at Monowitz (Auschwitz III), where he was put to work as a nurse in the camp hospital. After becoming ill himself, he was sent to the Auschwitz I (*Stammlager*) hospital where, after about a week, a parcel containing a note and a sardine sandwich arrived for him from Nora, who had been told of his arrival in the camp. She informed him that she was in Block 10.[52] Micheels interprets Nora's reappearance as an occurrence "that could not have been more evocative of […] Oedipal wishes and fantasies." That is to say, Nora became for him "the ideal woman, who in reality was sexually out of reach," a fact that "further enhanced the fairytale nature of the relationship."[53]

Micheels' account is, like de Wind's and Cohen's, somewhat at odds with his theory of survival. Like them, he confirms the importance of close relationships, especially in small groups.[54] His renewed contact with Nora is especially significant; echoing de Wind's story of "Hans'" contact with Friedel, Micheels explains how he was smuggled into Block 10 and how miraculous it was in Auschwitz that a couple should be reunited in this way.[55] Micheels reserves especially high praise for his friend Paul, the Blockältester, who helped smuggle him into Nora's block and kept a lookout whilst he was there, saying that "even in Auschwitz one could find true altruism."[56] Like de Wind, Micheels stresses that these friendships were crucial: "Such a bond was essential as a protection against losing all traces of civilized behaviour, and with them a true sense of hope and reason for survival."[57] And at one point, Micheels refers to another Dutch physician called Ed, working in Block 9. From Ed's ward in Block 9, he could look out of the window into Nora's room and wave at her.[58]

After the war, Micheels immigrated to the US, where he became a practicing psychoanalyst and clinical professor in psychiatry at Yale. He and Nora were reunited in June 1945 in Amsterdam but, a few months later,

---

[52] Micheels, *Doctor #117641*, 74–75.
[53] Micheels, *Doctor #117641*, 191.
[54] Micheels, *Doctor #117641*, 54.
[55] Micheels, *Doctor #117641*, 76–77.
[56] Micheels, *Doctor #117641*, 78.
[57] Micheels, *Doctor #117641*, 81. See also 184: "during the war and life in the camps it was essential to have a few close and trusted friends with whom to share such secrets."
[58] Micheels, *Doctor #117641*, 89.

they separated. Nora had not expected Micheels to survive and this fact hurt him, as Micheels felt that "it took some unusual fortitude to accomplish this and that she had surmised I did not possess this special ingredient."[59] For his part, Micheels surmised years later, "I am convinced that another important factor contributing to our parting grew out of my desire to forget the immediate past."[60] When he published his memoir at the age of 72 in 1989, he drew on years of psychoanalytic work to try and explain his own survival. Although he stated somewhat vaguely that "personality traits" like "an instinct for survival" made a difference, Micheels also echoed de Wind in noting that "I found that making myself inconspicuous might help me avoid trouble."[61] Micheels also appeals directly to psychoanalytic concepts; he notes, for example, that the gloves made for him by Nora that he wore during the death march provided a "bonding process" that "helped preserve a healthy amount of secondary-process thinking as a check on primary-process incursions." In other words, the gloves "represented her and the meaning of our relationship as very real in contrast with the intruding fantasies or mirages. As a result I woke up immediately."[62] What we see in Micheels' account is, like de Wind's and Cohen's, a theory of survival that does not wholly concur with his account of his own experiences. Micheels emphasizes inconspicuousness in a way that is similar to de Wind's "stupor" but it is clear that he also worked hard on sustaining close friendships and, above all, his (real and imagined) relationship with Nora, the "magic quality" of which "provided me with a sense of protection or immunity that sustained me through many harrowing experiences."[63] And, Micheels says, "I realized that as a doctor-nurse I was sort of upper-middle class in the camp society."[64] Indeed, the fact that all three men were doctors, at least nominally able to practice their craft—however imperfectly—in Auschwitz, gave them not just a sense of purpose but access to resources and a status that by no means overrode the role of

---

[59] Micheels, *Doctor #117641*, 192.
[60] Micheels, *Doctor #117641*, 195.
[61] Micheels, *Doctor #117641*, 84.
[62] Micheels, *Doctor #117641*, 185.
[63] Micheels, *Doctor #117641*, 191.
[64] Micheels, *Doctor #117641*, 84. On Micheels, see also Ron Rosenbaum, *Explaining Hitler: The Search for the Origins of His Evil* (London: Macmillan, 1998), ch15; Ross W. Halpin, *Jewish Doctors and the Holocaust: The Anatomy of Survival in Auschwitz* (Berlin: De Gruyter, 2018), 40–55.

luck but made their luck just a little less capricious than the average inmate's.

Conclusions

To what extent can the claims put forward in these three accounts of survival be put down to the authors being Dutch? Yehudi Lindeman writes of Cohen that he "views human identity as looser, more changeable and less ruled by ethical imperatives" than does Primo Levi, who tends to critically moralize about himself and others.[65] He also notes the same openness as Cohen in the writings of Gerhard Durlacher, another Dutch survivor physician.[66] Yet, their national background is only part of the story; apart from the specifics of their experiences, class, political identification, and gender play a role. But as with attempts to find the "altruistic personality" or its opposite, the "authoritarian personality," there will always be some ingredient that accounts for an individual's behavior that we cannot put our finger on. Besides, providing an account of survival is of course not the same as surviving; whatever their personal traits, the psychologist-survivors discussed here all survived—as they admit to a greater or lesser extent—through luck. Even if adopting a kind of "stupor" was a sine qua non—and we would be wise not to make this a universal condition—there will undoubtedly have been many inmates who took this stance but did not survive. Without luck, nothing was possible.

We should thus be cautious in confirming, as Benner, Roskies, and Lazarus wrote over 40 years ago, that "denial and *selective apathy* were keys to survival. With active denial and selective apathy, cognitive appraisals continued but they were reduced to bare essentials. The persecutees could not survive if their appraisals were not adjusted downward to basic

---

[65] Lindeman, "Abandonment, Adjustment, and Memory", 92.

[66] Another example is Jacques Tas, a Dutch psychotherapist who worked as a therapist in Belsen; I do not discuss him here because the circumstances in Belsen were markedly different from Auschwitz. See J. Tas, "Psychical Disorders among Inmates of Concentration Camps and Repatriates", *The Psychiatric Quarterly*, 25:4 (1951), 679–690. It is worth noting, however, that Tas writes (689) that being in the concentration camp led to "an immense accumulation and bottling up of sentiments of anxiety, rage, and aggressiveness ... This factor of suppressed and encapsulated aggressiveness, and the frequent ensuing repression of every affect, certainly can often explain the phenomenon in which psychic disturbances arising from a stay in a camp frequently come to light only months or even years after the return home."

survival issues. ... Only those who could engage in selective apathy and active denial survived."[67] Or, as the author of an article in the Polish *Przegląd Lekarski—Oświęcim* noted in 1970: "Suppression was the usual defence mechanism then. It enabled the prisoners to survive the most critical period."[68] "Selective apathy," "suppression," or what Emil Utitz called "living provisionally" [*das Provisorische*], is what de Wind calls "stupor." Wanting to survive and having a "rich inner life" is on its own an unsatisfactory explanation, for there were unquestionably many murdered who had such resources. Those who survived did so primarily through luck and then through allowing themselves to adjust their expectations downward to get through each day. Nevertheless, it is undeniable that some of the most powerful accounts of survival that we have come from individuals who devoted themselves to caring for others, had a network of friends and a rich spiritual life, understood in the broadest sense. We will see examples of this sort in Chap. 3.

A great reversal took place in psychoanalysis with the formulation of the concept of trauma. Freud had begun with a version of trauma derived from the sexual abuse (or as he put it, seduction) of children, and later placed greater emphasis on phantasy. Thus, although the notion of trauma caused by external events lay at the foundations of psychoanalysis, after the war, it was still *de rigueur* to argue that psychic illnesses stemmed from childhood disturbances. As late as 1972, de Wind felt obliged to note that:

> Some of the experts among the German rehabilitation authorities were terribly wrong when they considered infantile neurosis to be the cause of the illness that followed after the war. Most of the prisoners were well balanced psychically until the war; the infantile neurosis only influenced the victims' reaction pattern. This denial that persecution was the cause of the last

---

[67] Patricia Benner, Ethel Roskies, and Richard S. Lazarus, "Stress and Coping under Extreme Conditions", in Joel E. Dimsdale, M.D. (ed.), *Survivors, Victims, and Perpetrators: Essays on the Nazi Holocaust* (Washington: Hemisphere Publishing Corporation, 1980), 235.

[68] Piotr Wesełucha, "The Concentration Camp as a Psychiatric Experiment", *Przegląd Lekarski—Oświęcim*, 1970; *Medical Review Auschwitz*, 2017: https://www.mp.pl/auschwitz/journal/english/170032,the-concentration-camp-as-a-psychiatric-experiment

sequelae may well be inspired by the wish to minimize the enormous guilt of Nazi Germany.[69]

He was confirming what Krystal and Niederland had written a few years earlier when, in response to studies such as those conducted by émigré analyst Hans Strauss, who argued that survivors of Nazi persecution had a lower rate of mental illnesses than the population of New York, they noted that "we are confronted with the illogical conclusion that people's mental health is improved by persecution."[70]

Today, by contrast, at least according to psychologist Nathalie Zajde, "The trauma of concentration camp survivors has [...] become the paradigmatic case of all psychic trauma."[71] This is not the place to recapitulate Zajde's claim that what was once called "concentration camp syndrome" has been redefined since 1980 (with its first codification in the DSM-III) as PTSD with the result that the specific suffering of the Nazis' victims has been occluded in favor of a supposedly universally applicable diagnosis for all trauma-related suffering. Nor is this the place to pass judgement on claims such as Lomranz's, that the focus on psychopathological suffering and the overuse of the term "survivor" produces a "bulldozer effect" that "prevents both differentiation and changing impact of the trauma across the life span."[72] But if Zajde is right, it matters a great deal to which accounts of survival we give credence.

Both Bettelheim and Frankl, even if we grant that they, especially Bettelheim, stressed the importance of luck, favored an explanation that placed store on the victim's will to live, their being able to draw on inner resources. As we have seen, for de Wind, Micheels, and Cohen, and, I argue in the next chapter, implicitly backed up by the accounts of Lorska,

---

[69] de Wind, "Persecution, Aggression and Therapy", 176. For further discussion of this problem, see Dagmar Herzog, "The Obscenity of Objectivity: Post-Holocaust Anti-Semitism and the Invention-Discovery of Post-Traumatic Stress Disorder," in Wendy Lower and Lauren Faulkner Rossi (eds.), *Lessons and Legacies, Vol. XII: New Directions in Holocaust Research and Education* (Evanston: Northwestern University Press, 2017), 31–63; Herzog, *Cold War Freud: Psychoanalysis in an Age of Catastrophes* (Cambridge: Cambridge University Press, 2017), 215–216.

[70] Krystal and Niederland, "Clinical Observations on the Survivor Syndrome," 341. As Herzog notes (*Cold War Freud*, 103), Strauss became "a favourite" of the West German authorities.

[71] Nathalie Zajde, "The Psychiatric Treatment of Holocaust Survivors, or, the Tribulations of a Syndrome", in Dreyfus and Langton (eds.), *Writing the Holocaust*, 63.

[72] Lomranz, "The Skewed Effect", 50.

Brewda, Hautval, and Lingens-Reiner, which are about as far from Bettelheim's and Frankl's selective accounts of camp life as it possible to be, survival was less to do with the inmate's inner resources than his or her ability to enter a stupor-like state in which acceptance of reality maintained a delicate balancing act with not surrendering. Micheels expressed this clearly when he wrote that he knew of people who survived more than three years in the camps but who were killed in the final days of the war, people who, in his opinion, "had the essential ingredient, or a will to sustain life without which survival was impossible."[73] As Langer noted:

> The fact that 60,000 human beings—though their appearance at liberation belied this description—survived Auschwitz is less a triumph of the will than an accident of the body, combined with so many gratuitous and fortuitous circumstances that we will probably never be able to disentangle chance from choice, or relate effect to discernible cause.[74]

Merely the fact that de Wind's and Cohen's studies were published in the immediate postwar period is not enough to accord them analytical priority; after all, the first incarnation of *Man's Search for Meaning* was written (or dictated) in 1946 and Bettelheim's famous article on human behavior in extreme situations was published in 1943. Many of these studies opened by noting that, as Emil Utitz put it in 1948, "a great deal has been written on concentration camps in general and on Theresienstadt in particular."[75] De Wind himself opened his article of 1949, "Confrontation with Death," with the claim that "immediately after liberation, people were keen to read everything that was published about the concentration camps." He then went on: "The public devoured it all uncritically, but soon became sated."[76] A year later, Horkheimer and Flowerman's famous foreword to the *Studies in Prejudice* series, which included Adorno et al.'s *The Authoritarian Personality*, stated that "Today the world scarcely remembers the mechanized persecution and extermination of millions of

---

[73] Micheels, *Doctor #117641*, 193.
[74] Langer, *Versions of Survival*, 28.
[75] Emil Utitz, *Psychologie des Lebens im Konzentrationslager Theresienstadt* (Vienna: Verlag A. Sexl, 1948), 5.
[76] de Wind, "Confrontation with Death", 240.

human beings only a short span of years away in what was once regarded as the citadel of Western civilization."[77]

The fact that de Wind's book has been republished to great acclaim in many languages in the last few years—and despite the kitsch marketing, the text says what it says—speaks volumes about changing understanding of Holocaust "trauma." The acceptance of PTSD as a clinical diagnosis, for all the problems that have followed in its wake, shows that there is greater understanding of the fact, with respect to adults and, especially, children, that terrible situations leave long-lasting marks on a person's psychological being. Psychoanalysis has long lifted itself out of Freudian orthodoxy, the Freud-Klein wars, and other issues pertaining to the struggle for a universal explanation; the balance has shifted from placing the emphasis primarily on the "inner world" and "the question of the influence of unconscious phantasies on perceptions and the shaping of internal object relations" in favor of greater insistence on social and cultural circumstances.[78] This understanding does not mean that psychic reality is considered unimportant: Krystal and Niederland might have deliberately pushed too far with their arguments in order to change the compensation landscape. But it did make psychoanalysts more open to historical arguments. At the same time, historians have learned to differentiate the concentration camps from the death camps; to understand that the camps were always changing and that how a camp looked at the end of the war usually bore little relation to what it looked one, five, or (in the case of Dachau) twelve years earlier, and to navigate the complexities of camp "societies," which were also ever-changing.[79] It is perhaps no surprise that

[77] Max Horkheimer and Samuel H. Flowerman, "Foreword to Studies in Prejudice", in T. W. Adorno, Else Frenkel-Brunswik, Daniel J. Levinson and R. Nevitt Sanford, *The Authoritarian Personality*, abridged edn (New York: W.W. Norton & Company, 1982 [1950]), vii. See also Stephen Frosh, "Studies in Prejudice: Theorizing Anti-Semitism in the Wake of the Nazi Holocaust", in Matt ffytche and Daniel Pick (eds.), *Psychoanalysis in the Age of Totalitarianism* (London: Routledge, 2016), 29–41.
[78] Werner Bohleber, "Remembrance, Trauma, and Collective Memory: The Battle for Memory in Psychoanalysis", *International Journal of Psychoanalysis*, 88:2 (2007), 330. See also Emily A. Kuriloff, "The Holocaust and Psychoanalytic Theory and Practice", *Contemporary Psychoanalysis*, 46:3 (2010), 395–422; Kahn, *What Nazism Did to Psychoanalysis*; Alfred Garwood, *Holocaust Trauma and Psychic Deformation: Psychoanalytic Reflections of a Holocaust Survivor* (London: Routledge, 2021).
[79] Nikolaus Wachsmann, *KL: A History of the Nazi Concentration Camps* (London: Little, Brown, 2015); Dan Stone, *Fate Unknown: Tracing the Missing after World War II and the Holocaust* (Oxford: Oxford University Press, 2023).

a version of survival that stresses chance and existing in a kind of stupor rather than a will to live based on inner resources has come to assume greater persuasive strength.

Studies by Lomranz and others have shown that many (but not all) survivors were able to readjust to "normal" life in time, irrespective of the atrocious experiences they had endured.[80] There may well have been survivors who rebuilt their lives after the Holocaust by believing that they survived because they willed it. But for most, and closer to the reality of what we know about the camps, survival was above all a matter of luck, in which neither fighting the system not giving in to it was able to dominate the mind. It seems remarkable now that these inmate physicians articulated this in the immediate postwar period, not because of how short a time had passed to allow them to gather their thoughts, but because the intervening decades have been dominated by wishful thinking, mythologizing the camps and survival thereof, and forms of treatment that have not always been kind to the former camp inmates. The acceptance of the idea of massive social trauma, the formulation of PTSD, and its acceptance as a clinical diagnosis, the questioning of the monolithic concept of "survivor syndrome," and the realization that Holocaust survivors are human beings with frailties and strengths like all other people, have gradually created a situation where, in the scholarly if not the commemorative world, complexity and not myth-making prevail. Survival was not merely a matter of the individual's inner qualities, nor were the survivors' postwar lives determined solely by the Holocaust; in what reads today as a truism but in 1972 de Wind obviously felt needed to be said in the psychoanalytical journals, "Apart from the inner qualities of the survivors, a primary condition for their rehabilitation is to live in a world free from fear, injustice and authoritative coercion."[81] What de Wind and his colleagues teach us—and what they have been trying to teach us since 1945—is that the brutal reality of the Nazi crimes can only be understood when it is not idealized or turned into a manual for self-help.

---

[80] In addition to works cited above, see for example: Dov Shmotkin, Amit Shrira, Shira C. Goldberg, and Yuval Palgi, "Resilience and Vulnerability among Aging Holocaust Survivors and Their Families: An Intergenerational Overview", *Journal of Intergenerational Relationships*, 9:1 (2011), 7–21; Vera Békés, J. Christopher Parry, and Claire J. Starrs, "Resilience in Holocaust Survivors: A Study of Defense Mechanisms in Holocaust Narratives", *Journal of Aggression, Maltreatment and Trauma*, 26:10 (2017), 1072–1089.

[81] De Wind, "Persecution, Aggression and Therapy", 176.

CHAPTER 3

The Female Doctors of Block 10 in Auschwitz: Gender, Resistance, and Survival

Abstract One of the most noteworthy yet little-known markers of what we would today call "Holocaust consciousness" in Britain in the 1960s was the *Dering v. Uris* libel trial, in which former Polish inmate-physician of Auschwitz, Władysław Dering, sued American author Leon Uris for libel for comments he made about the number of operations Dering had performed in Auschwitz in his novel *Exodus*. The trial, held at the Royal Courts of Justice in London in 1964, attracted a good deal of attention in the press. Not the least reason for this attention was the remarkable testimony given by three women who had been inmate-physicians in Auschwitz, albeit in very different circumstances to Dering: Dorota Lorska, Alina Brewda, and Adélaïde Hautval. This chapter analyzes their testimony in the context of the trial itself and asks what their cross-examination tells us about the state of knowledge about the Holocaust in Britain at this period. It then goes on to ask what we can learn from their writings prior to and following the trial, considering issues of gender, resistance, inmate society, and solidarity in Auschwitz, and the question—much debated in the 1960s thanks to the writings of Viktor Frankl and Bruno Bettelheim—of what facilitated survival.

Keywords Auschwitz • Gender • Inmate-physicians • Resistance • Survival • Uris trial

The memoirs by de Wind, Micheels, and Cohen that I examined in Chap. 2 were of course written by men. They are, unsurprisingly, gendered texts; even though they did not reflect explicitly on their survival as a gendered phenomenon, they each spoke of their "privilege" in the camp, their relationships with other men, and, most revealingly, their relationships with their wives, in the case of de Wind and Micheels, and with the women in Block 10 and elsewhere in Auschwitz. In particular, each of the authors refers by name to several female inmate-physicians who, it turns out, were of exceptional importance to the other women in the block: Alina Brewda, Dorota Lorska (Slavka Kleinová), and Adélaïde Hautval. At first glance, it appears that we are faced with a classically gendered scenario, in which the women appear only insofar as they are named in texts by men. In fact, when one changes one's focus, the reverse can just as easily be true: the Dutch male psychoanalysts can be seen as having walk-on parts in the female inmate physicians' compelling and remarkable stories of survival.

In this chapter, I ask what we can learn about these women inmate doctors and test whether their theories of survival differ from or concur with those offered by the male Dutch psychoanalysts. We will see that the women concerned—physicians, not psychoanalysts—displayed the kind of independence that speaks less to de Wind's theory of "stupor" than to Frankl's and Bettelheim's theory of "rich inner life." Even if the occasion of the women giving testimony at the *Dering v. Uris* libel trial in London in 1964 created a kind of heroic story about them, giving them a mythic aura, they undoubtedly displayed extraordinary bravery during their time in Auschwitz for which they are rightly remembered.[1] Their stories are exceptional, not just because they demonstrate the power of spiritual resources, but because they were placed in a position where they could use those resources. That is to say, even these exceptional women survived to a large extent through "luck." Besides, their own explanations are quite divorced from the later heroic narratives that were ascribed to them; indeed, they are, as we will see, rather sober and bleak.

One quickly learns that, like their male counterparts de Wind, Micheels, and Cohen, the female inmate doctors in Block 10 who are named in the men's texts provided equally somber and practical assessments of survival. These women, especially the above-mentioned Brewda, Lorska, and

---

[1] I discuss the Uris/Dering libel trial below but see also my "Female Inmate-Physicians of Block 10 at Auschwitz as Witnesses at the Dering v. Uris Libel Trial", in *Britain and Holocaust Consciousness in the 1960s*, eds. Johannes-Dieter Steinert and Dan Stone (London: Bloomsbury, 2025); and Johannes-Dieter Steinert, *Dering v. Uris: Britain Encounters the Holocaust in the Sixties* (forthcoming).

Hautval, but also Ella Lingens-Reiner, have largely been overlooked in the English-language historiography, by comparison with their Jewish counterparts in Auschwitz, such as Gisella Perl, Lucie Adelsberger, or Olga Lengyel.[2] Yet, Lingens-Reiner, whose important book *Prisoners of Fear* (1948) has inexplicably been out of print for decades, was co-editor with Hermann Langbein and H.G. Adler of the German standard work *Auschwitz: Zeugnisse und Berichte* (first edition 1962); although not a qualified doctor, she functioned as one in Auschwitz. Hautval, whose narrative is hailed as a case of exemplary righteousness in the face of Nazi medical evil, has schools and streets in her native Alsace named after her and her 1946 memoir *Déportation* has been republished in French along with other of her works; Lorska has been the subject of several Polish studies, and was awarded the *Croix de Guerre* for her heroic behavior, and Brewda, the only one of the four who was Jewish, was appointed head physician of Block 10 by chief SS doctor Wirths in 1943,[3] and was the focus of a popular account (complete with a lurid, sexist cover very much of its time) published in 1966.[4] The latter three testified at the *Uris v. Dering* libel trial in London in 1964, which probably accounts for the publication shortly afterwards of the story of Brewda's time at Auschwitz; Dering was perhaps also one of the inspirations, along with Adolf Eichmann, for Karl Braun, alias Dr. Otto Reitmüller, the protagonist of Emeric Pressburger's 1966 novel *The Glass Pearls*.[5]

In this chapter, I analyze how the Block 10 women's positions in the camp allowed them to undertake forms of resistance that might not have been available to others.[6] But given my focus on psychoanalytical theories of survival, my main interest here is what the female doctors have to say about survival in Auschwitz. First, it is important to say something about gender and this chapter's focus on the female inmate physicians before

---

[2] Gisella Perl, *I Was a Doctor in Auschwitz* (New York: International Universities Press, 1948); Lucie Adelsberger, *Auschwitz: A Doctor's Story* (London: Robson, 1996); Olga Lengyel, *Five Chimneys: The Story of Auschwitz*. See Sari J. Siegel, "The Past and Promise of Jewish Prisoner-Physicians' Accounts", *SIMON: Shoah: Intervention, Methods, Documentation*, 3:1 (2016), 89–103, for discussion.

[3] Claude Romney, "Jewish Medical Resistance in Block 10, Auschwitz," in Michael A. Grodin (ed.), *Jewish Medical Resistance in the Holocaust* (New York: Berghahn Books, 2014), 188.

[4] R. J. Minney, *I Shall Fear No Evil: The Story of Alina Brewda's Survival in Auschwitz* (London: Corgi, 1968 [1966]). See also Ross W. Halpin, *Jewish Doctors and the Holocaust: The Anatomy of Survival in Auschwitz* (Berlin: De Gruyter, 2018), 91–97.

[5] Emeric Pressburger, *The Glass Pearls* (London: Faber & Faber, 2022).

[6] For a brief survey, see Romney, "Jewish Medical Resistance."

proceeding. It is well established by historians of gender that men's narratives of survival tend to focus on themselves whereas women's tend to focus on relationships.[7] The writings of de Wind, Micheels, and Cohen cannot entirely be categorized in this way, however. They are about themselves but the roles played by their wives (in de Wind's and Micheels' cases) and by other women, especially the inmate physicians, is by no means left in the shadows as is often the case in men's accounts.[8] Nevertheless, when it comes to the women who are the focus of this chapter, my interest in them here derives from the fact that they do not receive the full attention they deserve in the Dutchmen's texts.

A bigger problem than giving the women their rightfully deserved acknowledgement as historical actors arises, however, when one considers the roles they played in Block 10. Much recent work on sexual violence in the Holocaust and on female perpetrators in particular seeks to "unmask" female behavior that is considered "deviant." That is to say, the "discovery" that women also had the capacity for deeds considered "evil" and usually figured as the preserve of men might tend not just to "equalize" the sexes but to play into a vulgar stereotype of women who do not conform to gender norms. In considering this work, Karyn Ball wonders whether this "unmasking" engages in "inadvertent complicity" with sexual perversity. Ball asks whether "a feminist scholarly agenda calling for attention to the gendered and sexual differentiation of historical experiences colludes with this will in sexualizing the untold and therefore 'secret' horrors of the Holocaust."[9] The focus here, however, is not on female perpetrators but female victims who have been portrayed and understood

---

[7] Marion Kaplan, "Gender: A Crucial Tool in Holocaust Research", in Larry V. Thompson (ed.), *Lessons and Legacies, Vol. IV: Reflections on Religion, Justice, Sexuality, and Genocide* (Evanston, IL: Northwestern University Press, 2003), 163–170.

[8] Kaplan ("Gender", 166–167) refers to Victor Klemperer's diary as an example.

[9] Karyn Ball, *Disciplining the Holocaust* (Albany: SUNY Press, 2008), 195. See also Susannah Heschel, "Does Atrocity Have a Gender? Feminist Interpretations of Women in the SS", in Jeffry M. Diefendorf (ed.), *Lessons and Legacies, Vol. VI: New Currents in Holocaust Research* (Evanston: Northwestern University Press, 2004), 300–321; Doris L. Bergen, "Sexual Violence in the Holocaust: Unique and Typical?", in Dagmar Herzog (ed.), *Lessons and Legacies, Vol. VII: The Holocaust in International Perspective* (Evanston: Northwestern University Press, 2006), 179–200. Heschel writes (315), "Feminist theory has tended to portray women evil-doers as having entered a male realm" and argues instead (317) that "Volunteering at a concentration camp, then, would not be an indication of women as 'male imitators', but an expression of aspects of the peculiar femininity endorsed by the Nazi regime."

as "heroic." The risk is the mirror opposite to that set out by Ball: not sexualizing these women's histories but making their gender identity in itself cause for celebration. That is to say, an ostensibly feminist agenda celebrating the women's behavior and ending up reinforcing conventional notions of women's roles as carers and sharers (and men's as self-centered individualists), in a way that can be perceived as inimical to the critical impetus that gave rise to such studies in the first place.

The problem is that the context of Block 10 means that there is inevitably a sexual aspect to this history, in that the women were helping other female inmates (many still teenage girls) who were having ovaries removed without their consent in experimental sterilization operations. The setting is lurid and open to sensationalist abuse; thus, it is crucial neither to tarry with the perversion embodied by the SS doctors, nor to engage in hagiographical celebrations. At the same time, it is imperative to acknowledge the women individually and not only as representatives of a larger group. According to Michael Nutkiewicz:

> The public dehumanization of the Jews was the reversal of most trauma victims' experience (rape or incest) in contemporary society. During the Holocaust Jews endured a corporate rape that took place in public space. Just as rape in the private space elicits the sense of having been dishonored, and thus violated morally, physical assault in the public arena was meant to dishonor the corporate body and thus violate the Jewish people morally. Every survivor was witness to this collective assault, and at one time or another its victim.[10]

While in some ways obviously true, this sort of statement overlooks— or has the potential to overlook—the specific suffering of individuals, and the actual rape or other sexual abuse that they suffered. The use of rape as a metaphor is problematic here insofar as it permits us to avoid thinking about actual rape or sexual violence as part of the history of the Holocaust.[11]

Who were these women? The three who testified in the *Dering v. Uris* trial were obviously exceptional individuals; the two law reporters who wrote the account of the trial dedicated their book to the "three women

---

[10] Michael Nutkiewicz, "Shame, Guilt, and Anguish in Holocaust Survivor Testimony," *Oral History Review*, 30:1 (2003), 5.

[11] For a discussion of this problem in a different context, see Ruth Harris, "The 'Child of the Barbarian': Rape, Race and Nationalism in France during the First World War", *Past and Present*, 141 (1993), 170–206.

doctors" who were "Prisoners in Block 10, Auschwitz 1943." This seems quite startling, when one considers that the book is offered as a sober, dispassionate account of the trial, with no partisan commentary on the part of the authors. Yet, the fact that Hill and Williams chose to dedicate the book to the three women immediately positions them and indicates where their sympathies lie. At the trial itself, the women each gave testimony that first and foremost contradicted the claims of Dr. Dering and his lawyers, leaving the jury with the difficult task—especially in Brewda's case—of weighing up two irreconcilable versions of what had transpired in Block 10. Their words, moreover, left the jury and everyone else present astounded at their bravery and the dignity with which they spoke. We will return to the trial shortly but let us first see how the women are discussed in the Dutchmen's accounts.

Brewda is referred to in de Wind's account in the context of a discussion with his wife Friedel that took place in Block 10 concerning an argument between the SS doctor Clauberg and his assistant, the inmate physician Maximilian Samuel. The latter proposed protecting 40 "deserving" women who worked in the block from Clauberg's experiments, and the argument had been repeated between Clauberg's assistant, Sylvia, and Brewda.[12] After de Wind asked who the latter was, Friedel explain to him that Brewda was "Our current Blockälteste. She's a doctor, but she sabotages the experiments when she can."[13] On returning to Block 9, Hans discusses what Friedel has told him with Klempfner, a Czech doctor who had been in various camps for four years and "knew the ins and outs."[14] Klempfner thought that using the staff for experiments—which is what he assumed would happen if Samuel were removed—would be the lesser of two evils: "They're better off getting an injection than being sent to Birkenau. Those experiments aren't that terrible." Hans agreed than "anything was better than Birkenau" but "couldn't go along with his opinion that the experiments 'weren't that terrible.'"[15] Hans replies: "Even if they only harm a single hair on those women's heads, it's still as bad a crime as

---

[12] See Sari J. Siegel, "Treating an Auschwitz Prisoner-Physician: The Case of Dr. Maximilian Samuel," *Holocaust and Genocide Studies*, 28:3 (2014), 450–481; Adélaïde Hautval, *Médicine et crimes contre l'humanité: témoignage* (Arles: Actes Sud, 1991), 79–80, who says that Dr. Samuel obeyed the Nazis out of fear and in the hope that his daughter, who was also in the camp, would be saved.
[13] de Wind, *Last Stop Auschwitz*, 114.
[14] de Wind, *Last Stop Auschwitz*, 112.
[15] de Wind, *Last Stop Auschwitz*, 115.

a major operation, because the nature of the crime is not determined by the seriousness of the experiment, but by the compulsion under which it is carried out."[16] Hans's claims (and the philosophical nature of the discussion in Block 9 in Auschwitz is noteworthy in itself) are later backed up by another inmate physician, Professor Mansfeld, who condemns German science as going against "every human principle," and who assures Hans that "If one of my former lab assistants had treated a laboratory animal the way the women are treated here, I would have marched him to the door myself."[17]

Towards the end of the war, as the tension in the camp rose, Hans was moved to Block 19; Friedel was moved to Block 23, where she worked as a nurse. One evening, Brewda turned up with a female patient in need of an operation and now Hans recognizes her key role in the camp: "For half a year she had been the Blockälteste of Block 10—until she had refused to cooperate with a particular experiment." She is also referred to as "Friedel's guardian angel" whom he could trust. At this point in time, with the evacuation of the camp and the end of the war—but not the freedom of its inmates—in sight, Brewda was "in a dark mood. She had seen too much."[18] This picture of Brewda as a stalwart resister and realistic assessor of camp conditions is consistent with those of Hautval and Lorska, both of whom appear as archetypes of moral steadfastness in the face of overwhelming evil. Indeed, after the war, Brewda wrote in a way that confirmed what de Wind and Mansfeld said:

> If someone says to me today that Dr Clauberg was a scientist, a researcher or a university teacher, I simply cannot understand it. If I think about the fact that he carried out his experiments on women who found themselves in the concentration camp and who were unable freely to offer their consent, I cannot make that mesh with the image of a doctor, who should be a helper, or of a university teacher, who should be a role model for the young, for such a man is either an opportunist [*Karrierejaeger*] or a criminal.[19]

---

[16] de Wind, *Last Stop Auschwitz*, 115.
[17] de Wind, *Last Stop Auschwitz*, 150.
[18] de Wind, *Last Stop Auschwitz*, 166.
[19] Alina Brewda, "A Jewish Woman-Doctor in the Clauberg-Block", Wiener Holocaust Library, P.III.h (Auschwitz), No. 1061 (1959), 12. The title page is in English but the text is in German. Also "Dr. Dering Libelled", *BMJ* (16 May 1964), 1321–1323.

Like Brewda, Hautval refers to Clauberg with contempt. Indeed, she refers to him simply as "le 'professeur Clauberg.'"[20] In return, Hautval is recalled for her exemplary behavior. According to Hermann Langbein, one of the leaders of the underground movement in Auschwitz: "Although the list of doctors who refused to carry out the orders of the SS and did their sworn duty even in Nazi concentration camps is bound to remain incomplete, it must include the name of the French physician Adelaide Hautval, who openly refused to participate in the pseudomedical experiments of the SS in Auschwitz."[21]

Hautval is not referred to in de Wind's text but is mentioned by Micheels. He mentions her in an article entitled "Bearers of the Secret" which seeks to understand the psychological barriers to understanding the Holocaust. Hautval is offered as an important example of how one could become a *Geheimnisträger* ("bearer of the secret," i.e., one who knew what was happening at Auschwitz), thus condemned to die, and cope with that knowledge. "The only way out of this position and the associated sense of guilt (if simply for being a silent witness)," according to Micheels:

> was to refuse to assist the SS in any form or manner in their criminal activities. A non-Jewish French doctor, Adelaide Hautval, refused to assist the SS doctors in their sterilization experiments. She was very explicit in saying "no" to Wirths. He could not understand her human concern for such "lowly creatures as Jews". Although she lost her prominent and relatively privileged position, she did manage to survive. Had she been Jewish, survival would not have been possible.[22]

Micheels' final statement is questionable but what matters here is the respect for Hautval that comes through, and which Micheels provides in contrast to the many examples he gives of survivors who were psychologically damaged by their experiences, himself included. Cohen, by contrast, cites both Hautval and Lorska as two among a number of authorities on the sterilization experiments, but apart from noting that Hautval was sent to Birkenau from Block 10 in July 1943 for refusing to take part in the experiments, he has nothing to say about either of them specifically.[23]

By contrast with how they are spoken about by the men, which is respectful but in a carefully circumscribed way, the women talk about each

---

[20] Hautval, *Médicines*, 75.
[21] Hermann Langbein, *Against All Hope: Resistance in the Nazi Concentration Camps 1938–1945* (London: Constable, 1994), 169.
[22] Louis J. Micheels, "Bearer of the Secret", *Psychoanalytic Inquiry*, 5:1 (1985), 23.
[23] See Cohen, *Human Behaviour in the Concentration Camp*, 100.

other in glowing terms. For example, Lorska discusses Hautval as a paragon of virtue in an article she wrote for *Przegląd Lekarski*, or the postwar Auschwitz medical reports:

> Dr Hautval was the model of a doctor, who fulfilled her duties like a calling under all conditions, especially under the most difficult conditions. This uncommonly modest and noble woman assessed the situation in the camp with great sobriety. It was she who explained to me, in the first days after my arrival, about the SS doctors' activities in Block 10. She also made it clear to me that nothing would save us from having been witnesses to the crimes committed by the SS doctors, and that they would do everything to prevent the world from finding out what they had done.[24]

Brewda, in turn, mentioned Lorska, referring to her using her then married name of Dorota Kleinová, as having looked after her when she was sent to Block 10 in September 1943. At that point, "There had been no woman doctor in charge of Block 10 since Dr. Hautval had left a few weeks earlier."[25] Lorska, a communist who had served as a doctor with the International Brigades in Spain and had worked for the French Resistance from the start of the occupation, spoke to Brewda about the underground movement in Auschwitz. This consisted of women who had been arrested in France with Lorska and who were still together in Block 10, and was part of a wider network, the Auschwitz Fighting Group, of which Hermann Langbein (who also testified in the Dering trial) is perhaps the best-known member.[26] Brewda joined them and, through her friendship with Langbein, was able to obtain medicines for the women in Block 10.[27] Towards the end of the war, having been separated for several months (Brewda in Birkenau, Lorska in Auschwitz I), Brewda and Lorska were reunited and, when the camp was evacuated in January 1945, made the decision to try

---

[24] Dorota Lorska, "Block 10 in Auschwitz", in Hamburger Institut für Sozialforschung (ed.), *Die Auschwitz-Hefte. Vol. 1: Texte der polnischen Zeitschrift "Przegląd Lekarski" über historische, psychische und medizinische Aspekte des Lebens und Sterbens in Auschwitz* (Hamburg: Rogner & Bernhard Verlag), 212. See also Lorska, "My Time in Auschwitz", trans. Łukasz Mrozik, *Medical Review—Auschwitz* (15 December 2022), orig. *Przegląd Lekarski—Oświęcim* (1967), 206–208, online at: https://www.mp.pl/auschwitz/journal/english/313336,my-time-in-auschwitz

[25] R. J. Minney, *I Shall Fear No Evil* (London: Corgi, 1967), 117.

[26] See Hermann Langbein, *People in Auschwitz*.

[27] Minney, *I Shall Fear No Evil*, 143–146. See also Dr. Alina Bialostocka (née Brewda) in Lore Shelley (ed.), *Criminal Experiments on Human Beings in Auschwitz and War Research Laboratories: Twenty Women Prisoners' Accounts* (San Francisco: Mellen University Research Press, 1991), 39.

and stay behind together with the sick. However, they were found hiding and forced to join the evacuation columns, on which the two women, both ill, were helped along by several stronger inmates. At Wadowice they were put on board a train—an open carriage—and sent to Ravensbrück, and then, some days later, on to the sub-camp of Neustadt-Glewe. Eventually, both women were taken on as doctors in the camp hospital, where they still were when the Red Army arrived at the camp on 8 May.

DERING V. URIS

Although Brewda, Lorska, and Hautval each published their own writings after the war and each, to varying degrees, is reasonably well known in their countries of origin, it was the *Dering v. Uris* trial of April–May 1964 in London that brought them to international prominence. Soon after Leon Uris published his bestselling novel *Exodus*, he and his publishers were surprised to learn that they were being accused of libeling one Władysław Alexander Dering, a Polish doctor. In a few pages of his long novel, Uris describes how 17,000 operations were carried out in Auschwitz in 1943 by a "Dr Dehring." These operations, Uris wrote, were conducted on male and female Jewish "human guinea pigs" with the aim of finding ways to sterilize human beings on a large scale. Indeed, he wrote that Dehring "performed seventeen thousand 'experiments' in surgery without anaesthetic." Uris had not known that Dering was not only still alive but living and practicing in Finsbury Park in London. Given the setting of the experiments in the most notorious of Nazi camps, it was hardly surprising that Dering's assertions and the subsequent trial attracted considerable attention. As the authors of the trial report, Mavis Hill and L. Norman Williams, noted:

> The issues raised by the trial went far beyond the right of a man to claim compensation for damage done to his reputation by the publication of a defamatory statement; they pose for everybody basic questions of morals and ethics and human behaviour in adversity.[28]

The defendants did not seek to justify the figure of 17,000 operations, nor did they claim that the operations were carried out entirely without

---

[28] Mavis M. Hill and L. Norman Williams, *Auschwitz in England: A Record of a Libel Action* (London: MacGibbon & Kee, 1965), 15.

anesthetic. But, with the aid of a surviving logbook from the camp, held by the Auschwitz Museum, Uris' lawyers argued that Dering's own handwriting showed that he had performed sterilization operations—removing testicles or ovaries—from 130 Jewish adolescents between March and November 1943. They argued that even if the operations were not carried out entirely without anesthetic, Dering administered only a hastily delivered spinal anesthetic and no pre-medical treatment, meaning that the inmates were conscious throughout a procedure that was forced upon them. Dering's lawyers argued that such criticisms entirely misunderstood the nature of Auschwitz in 1943: Dering did the best he could under conditions where he was forced to carry out the operations by the SS, where there was a lack of hygiene and equipment of all sorts, and where he did not dispose of a staff of nurses to assist him. After a three-week trial, the jury found in favor of Dering but awarded him a halfpenny in damages, implying that although they agreed that Uris had inaccurately portrayed him and the extent of his activities, they probably believed that Dering had voluntarily performed gruesome operations in Auschwitz on Jewish men and women, without their consent, causing them immense physical and psychological harm. At the very least, the award signaled the jury's distaste for Dering's behavior, even if no specific facts were named. Although Dering had formally won the case, the £500 costs he was ordered to pay vastly outnumbered his 1/2d award, meaning that he was de facto, if not de jure, the case's loser, with his reputation substantially damaged. As Hautval observed, it was a civil trial that was virtually transformed into a war crimes trial.[29] It is hardly surprising that Uris went on to provide a loosely fictionalized account of the trial in *QBVII*; it was perfect material for a bestselling novel.

From today's perspective, perhaps the most striking thing about this little-known trial is that it questions many assumptions about how much was known about the Holocaust in postwar Britain. Recent scholarship shows that from the Nuremberg trials and exhibitions about the genocide of the Jews in the immediate postwar period to debates about the Palestine mandate and the emergence of Israel in the context of British detention of DPs in Germany and then in Cyprus, through to the Eichmann trial, as well as a wide range of reference in popular culture and the arts, there was

---

[29] Adélaïde Hautval, *Rester humain! Leçons d'Auschwitz et de Ravensbrück* (Paris: Editions Ampelos, 2018), 38 ("C'était un procès civil qui virtuellement s'est transformé en procès de criminel de guerre").

in fact considerable, if not systematic knowledge of what we would now call the Holocaust.[30] Nevertheless, one cannot talk about the kind of organized "Holocaust consciousness" that has existed since the 1990s in the UK, and thus there is something jarring about discovering a libel trial turning on the nature of the medical experiments conducted in Block 10 at Auschwitz in 1943 being held at the Royal Courts of Justice. Indeed, the title of the trial report—*Auschwitz in England*—and, when one reads it, the judge's comments, all indicate that the court took for granted at this moment in time what Auschwitz was and what happened there. The court case did not require, as did the *Irving v. Lipstadt* and Penguin Books libel case of 1999–2000, a lesson in the history of the Holocaust; rather, the plaintiff's and defendants' representatives got straight down to debating the intricacies of Block 10 and what happened there, assuming that the jury and the judge would be sufficiently well informed about what Auschwitz was.

Apart from the question of what the *Dering v. Uris* trial tells us about "Holocaust consciousness," one of the most significant things about it was the appearance of the female inmate physicians from Block 10. Their testimony electrified the courtroom and established them as the most remarkable of the witnesses. It is worth citing Hill and Williams at length, in their account of the judge's summing up. Reporting on the judge's summary of Lord Gardiner's argument for the defendants, Hill and Williams first note his claim that in 1943, Dering would not have been killed by the Nazis had he refused to conduct the operations, as they needed doctors to preserve the labor supply. Lord Gardiner then turned to the female inmate physicians to back up the claim:

> There was Dr Lorska in Block 10, who somehow avoided having to do any operations, though the Nazis knew she was a doctor. She said that punishments could be avoided, and there were ways of getting out of these things. There was Dr Brewda who said she had been faced with this problem and called on to help in Block 10 with particular experiments being done there, but dodged the issue by saying she had no experience of gynaecological surgery. Then there was Dr Hautval—perhaps one of the most impressive and courageous women who had ever given evidence in the courts of this

---

[30] For example: Christine Schmidt and Dan Stone, "Exhibiting the Missing: The World Jewish Congress' London Exhibition of 1947, 'Search for the Scattered'", *Journal of Holocaust Research*, 37:3 (2023), 297–316; David Cesarani and Eric J. Sundquist (eds.), *After the Holocaust: Challenging the Myth of Silence* (London: Routledge, 2012).

country, a most outstanding and distinguished person—and they knew what had happened to her. She had stood up to the Nazis four times, and made it quite clear at an early stage what she was prepared to do and what she was not prepared to do. ... So the jury were asked to infer that if Dr Dering had stood up, nothing would have happened to him.[31]

What was it that these three women said at the trial that made them the heroes of the court? And how does what they said in London and elsewhere relate to the discussion of survival in the previous chapter?

The trial followed the standard procedure: the barrister representing Dering, Mr. Colin Duncan, QC, and Lord Gardiner, Uris's leading counsel, opened the case to the jury together with the judge, Mr. Justice Lawton. The accusation of libel was explained, as was the meaning of the defense of justification. Dering gave his evidence in chief and was then cross-examined, then re-examined. Then the witnesses were called, beginning with those for the plaintiff. First came Dr. Christopher Hewer, a leading anesthetist. Then Mr. Duncan called a "surprise witness," Dr. Grabczynski, an inmate doctor with whom Dering had worked in Auschwitz and to whom Dering had referred on a number of occasions during his examination. Then followed the defendants' witnesses: a series of men and women who had been operated on by Dering at Auschwitz; the noted resistance leader and author Hermann Langbein; another inmate doctor, Stanislaw Klodzinski; Dr. John David Ebsworth, an anesthetist. Then came the doctors: Lorska; Brewda; two English doctors, William Nixon and Brian Windeyer, professors of obstetrics and gynecology and radiology, respectively; and, finally, Hautval.

Born in Poland, Brewda was now living in Brondesbury Park, London. Under the German occupation, Brewda had been incarcerated in the Warsaw Ghetto before being transported to Majdanek after the uprising of April 1943, and then to Auschwitz and Block 10 in September 1943. After a short time, Brewda was appointed medical chief of Block 10 by Wirths, in the full knowledge that despite being a "privileged" prisoner, she was condemned not to get out alive, just like all the other inmates. Brewda took upon herself the task of caring for the women in Block 10, noting that some, the Greek girls especially, "were really only children."[32] She learned that Dr. Dering, with whom she had been a medical student

---

[31] Hill and Williams, *Auschwitz in England*, 255.
[32] Hill and Williams, *Auschwitz in England*, 193.

in Warsaw when he was a houseman, was also in the camp, and sought him out, only to find him aloof and, for reasons she would soon learn, unfriendly.[33] Brewda was shocked by the speed at which Dering carried out ovariectomies in Block 10, on young Jewish women who were anesthetized from the waist down but who could observe what was being done to them and who had in any case not consented to the operations. When Brewda questioned what he was doing, Dering responded: "Shut up. I have my orders. They will kill me. I have to do it."[34] As Hautval later commented, "it is beyond doubt that Dering would not have treated his coreligionists in the same way."[35]

Unsurprisingly, the *Dering v. Uris* libel trial is a central focus of Minney's book on Brewda, which appeared not long after the trial. The mention of Brewda's encounter with Dering in Block 10 leads to a long discussion of the trial, which serves to frame Brewda's bravery in the camp. The witnesses—the women who had been operated on by Dering—all testified to her kindness, one saying that "If it had not been for Dr. Brewda I should not have lived."[36] Most important, the text then sets out why Dering's claim that he had no choice was undermined by the actions of Brewda, Lorska, and Hautval:

> Lord Gardiner pointed out that of the three women doctors in Block 10, Dr. Kleinova, after waiting six weeks as raw material for the experiments, had managed to join a laboratory in order to avoid having to perform such operations or becoming a victim herself as had at first seemed likely; Dr. Brewda had refused to respond to the requests made by Dr. Wirths and Dr. Schumann, but had heroically stood by the victims, had comforted them in their hour of suffering and had given them months of post-operative care; and Dr. Hautval had refused point blank to take part in any of these operations—and none of these three women doctors had been shot, indeed they were all alive and in court today.[37]

Much of Dering's case against Uris turned on whether he had performed as many operations as Uris had claimed, whether they could have been carried out properly given how quickly Dering did them, and, most

---

[33] Minney, *I Shall Fear No Evil*, 121–123.
[34] Minney, *I Shall Fear No Evil*, 129.
[35] Hautval, *Rester humain!*, 39.
[36] Minney, *I Shall Fear No Evil*, 132.
[37] Minney, *I Shall Fear No Evil*, 134.

important of all, whether or not he was obliged to perform them. Brewda, under questioning from Mr. Duncan, asserted that had Clauberg ordered her to remove a girl's ovary, she would never have done it: "I would try to invent some lies, as I did with Wirths and Schumann, and hope for the best. ... I knew many many doctors, and I never heard but one who did such things."[38] She reported that the speed with which Dering performed the operations meant that they could not have been done properly; proof of this claim was the condition the girls were in afterwards. Lorska made the same case, saying that the girls "did not heal in the usually accepted way."[39] And she pointed to Hautval as the prime example proving that inmates in Auschwitz could refuse the orders of the SS doctors.[40] Hautval's testimony, indeed, is startling for the boldness of her assertions and her moral clarity. It also speaks to the difference between physical survival (being alive at the moment of liberation) and long-term survival.[41] Hautval clearly did not expect to live to see the end of the Nazi regime and yet, over time, the reality of her life meant that she grappled with both of these forms of survival.

Both Minney's book and Hill and Williams' note that Hautval was the "most impressive witness"; "calm and composed," she explained how she had been asked to conduct operations by Wirths, how she initially accepted but, on seeing the condition of the women, refused to have any further role: "I saw Dr. Wirths again and told him that I could not do the work. He asked me my opinion on sterilisation and I answered that I was absolutely opposed to it. We had no right to dispose of the life and destiny of others."[42] In answer to Lord Gardiner, Hautval then explained that she was not punished for standing up to Wirths in this way, although from then on, she assumed that she would not get out of the camp alive. When Wirths asked her, "Cannot you see that these people are different from you?," she replied: "that there were several people different from me, starting with him." As the judge later noted, this was a "devastating reply which would live in the jury's memory for many years."[43]

[38] Hill and Williams, *Auschwitz in England*, 202.
[39] Hill and Williams, *Auschwitz in England*, 186.
[40] Hill and Williams, *Auschwitz in England*, 190.
[41] My thanks to Hank Greenspan for this distinction.
[42] Minney, *I Shall Fear No Evil*, 136.
[43] Minney, *I Shall Fear No Evil*, 137. See also Hill and Williams, *Auschwitz in England*, 219–224; Hans-Joachim Lang, *Die Frauen von Block 10: Medizinische Versuche in Auschwitz* (Augsburg: Weltbild, 2018), 175–182.

Brewda's, Lorska's, and Hautval's testimonies were the centerpiece of the trial and probably did more than anything to convince the jury that even if what Uris had written about Dering was incorrect, they did not believe his claim that he acted under duress. Nevertheless, somewhat like the "four women" who assisted the Auschwitz Sonderkommando in obtaining gunpowder to be used in the revolt at Birkenau, the female doctors of Block 10 have to a large extent been overlooked. The collective memory of the experiments carried out at Auschwitz has focused on the perpetrators and, to a lesser extent, on the (usually unnamed) victims.[44] To what extent can the women's claims about standing up to the Nazis and refusing to take part in the human experiments explain their survival?

Survival

In her memoir, published in 1948, Ella Lingens-Reiner explained that at first she thought that one should behave "properly" in the camps; she tells how she objected to a 70-year old female German political prisoner collecting wood to burn without permission:

> I was still under the impression that it was advisable for people in our situation to behave with exemplary correctness. To the very last I could not get rid of this notion, although it was quite absurd. In reality only those prisoners had a chance to survive in the camp—if they were not privileged on account of their profession, beauty, or other specially favourable circumstances—who were determined to do the exact opposite of what they were told to do, on principle to break every rule governing civilian life.[45]

As Langer observes of this passage, Lingens-Reiner indicates that those who tried to salvage the moral luggage of civilized values "imposed fatal burdens on themselves" because, as her description of the camps shows, we are confronted "by conditions that with very few exceptions *prohibit* the exercise of uncontaminated moral freedom and hence the achievement

---

[44] See Isabel Wollaston, "Emerging from the Shadows? The Auschwitz Sonderkommando and the 'Four Women' in History and Memory", *Holocaust Studies*, 20:3 (2014), 137–170, for a comparable project, although the women discussed by Wollaston were all murdered at Auschwitz. An exception to the tendency not to consider who the victims were is Paul Weindling, *Victims and Survivors of Nazi Human Experiments: Science and Suffering in the Holocaust* (London: Bloomsbury, 2015).

[45] Ella Lingens-Reiner, *Prisoners of Fear* (London: Victor Gollancz, 1948), 22.

of a tragic dignity to temper the austerity of human doom in Auschwitz."[46] Brewda's, Lorska's, and Hautval's testimony in London, however, provides an alternative reading. Their words and actions suggest that there was room—in certain circumstances—for "normal" ethical standards to function and to remain effective. At the very least, they represent examples of Langer's exceptions.

Called first to take the witness stand, Dorota Lorska explained how she had been deported from France, where she had been living since the late 1930s, having been born in Poland but married in Prague, where she had studied medicine. She was arrested as a member of the resistance and deported to Auschwitz on 2 August 1943. Having identified herself as a doctor when questioned on arrival, she was sent to Block 10, where she became acquainted with Hautval and, in September, with Brewda. Her testimony centers on her refusal to cooperate with the Germans in their experiments on the female inmates in the block, and Mr. Duncan's attempt to get the jury to respond to her claims with incredulity. Towards the end of his questioning, Duncan asked Lorska whether, had she been ordered to take part in experimental operations, she would have done so. Lorska, in response, asked the judge if she might say something, to which he gave his assent. She then said:

> In the first days of my stay in Block 10, one evening I spoke with Dr Hautval. This conversation took place in the operating theatre. She explained to me as a doctor what was happening in Block 10. At the end of that conversation she told me that it was impossible that we should ever get out of the camp alive. "The Germans will not allow people who know what is happening here to get into touch with the outside world," Dr Hautval said, "so the only thing that is left to us is to behave, for the rest of the short time that remains to us, as human beings." I have never forgotten that conversation, and in all the difficult moments of my life I have remembered what she said to me.[47]

She then claimed, before the questioning closed, that she would have committed suicide rather than cooperate, had she been ordered by Clauberg to remove a girl's ovary.

Lorska's words help us to understand Micheels' discussion of Hautval. Micheels' point is that women like Hautval—unlike many of

---

[46] Langer, *Versions of Survival*, 74 (emphasis in original).
[47] Hill and Williams, *Auschwitz in England*, 190.

his patients and, he seems to suggest, unlike himself—would not suffer from the psychic damage caused by repressing memories of humiliation and helplessness, since she had behaved (and, more to the point, had had the opportunity to behave) in a way that asserted her agency. For example:

> A middle-aged woman made it explicitly clear at the onset of her treatment that she would not talk about her war experiences. She preferred to struggle with recurrent severe depressions and anxiety attacks. She suffered from the latter whenever anybody in her immediate family packed a suitcase. An hour after her daughter packed a suitcase to return to college and drove away, the patient panicked. In therapy, she recalled that each member of her family had packed a suitcase in advance so as to be ready when the Nazis came to round them up. All of them, including her first husband, had perished. This patient interrupted her treatment after two months.[48]

In these accounts, we see survival facilitated by the women standing up for themselves, not allowing themselves to have their humanity destroyed by the Nazis. However, this is far too simple a conclusion.

It is worth considering Elie Cohen's argument here that survival was a matter of egotism. "In the concentration camp," writes Cohen, "man was beaten back to his most animal basis. His only concern was with that which would help to keep him alive. This was a regression to the primitive phase of the drive to self-preservation."[49] He goes on to argue that the superego—in simplest terms, the voice of the parents, in other words, the conscience—had to be silenced in order to survive in the concentration camps: "Theft, egotism, lack of consideration for others, pitilessness, disregarding of all laws, all this was prohibited in pre-concentration camp days; inside the concentration camp, however, it was normal."[50] He concludes that "The only restriction which still held the attempted satisfaction of the hunger drive in check, was the reality principle," that is, whether or not satisfying the hunger drive threatened the inmate's life; even then, given the extreme hunger from which camp inmates were suffering, this threat would only be taken into consideration insofar as it delayed the

---

[48] Micheels, "Bearer of the Secret", 27.
[49] Cohen, *Human Behaviour in the Concentration Camp*, 134.
[50] Cohen, *Human Behaviour in the Concentration Camp*, 137.

attempt to satisfy the hunger drive, "unless the drive was so powerful that it also blew the last fuse."[51]

An example of the drive to stay alive might be provided by the Auschwitz Sonderkommando. As Hautval wrote about them: "Outside, the Sonderkommando (in charge of the crematorium) laugh. They laugh when they see the half-corpses [*les demi-cadavres*] bouncing on the ground. They laugh, the unfortunates, no doubt so as not to cry in front of 'them.'"[52] De Wind's discussion with Professor Kabeli, written in 1945, is much less critical; in fact, it allows Kabeli to relate in a matter-of-fact manner what being a member of the Sonderkommando meant, and de Wind makes none of the negative judgements that became common currency later on. Hautval's words combine sympathy for the men with a kind of repulsion, a fear of getting too close to them. No doubt for a woman who had refused to take part in the Nazi experiments, the thought that the Sonderkommando men had performed their tasks—even knowing that they had not opted for the role—must have been hard for her to take. Her words also provide further insight into Hautval's—and by implication, the other women inmate doctors'—attitude towards her own survival. Paul Marcus notes, in his sympathetic analysis of Bettelheim's writings, that inmates with a degree of attitudinal freedom fared best:

> Bettelheim is emphasizing that to maintain a more or less coherent narrative of self-identity, some semblance of autonomy and integration, an inmate had to at least maintain some kind of decision-making capacity and attitudinal freedom, a sense that he was an actor in the world, "that [he] could, at any phase in a given sequence of conduct, have acted differently" if he chose to. [...] Thus, if the inmate was able to use a narrative in which he understood his compliance to the Nazis, not as absolute capitulation and degradation, but rather, as a necessary compromise in order to survive, then he still maintained some basic sense of himself as the same person he was prior to his incarceration.[53]

We are confronted in the accounts of Lingens-Reiner, Hautval, Lorska, and Brewda with a paradox: their words speak of the SS's brutality, often in matter-of-fact terms that are very hard to read. Their tales

---

[51] Cohen, *Human Behaviour in the Concentration Camp*, 138.
[52] Hautval, *Médicine et crimes contre l'humanité*, 42.
[53] Paul Marcus, *Autonomy in the Extreme Situation: Bruno Bettelheim, the Nazi Concentration Camps and the Mass Society* (Westport, CT: Praeger, 1999), 91–92.

are of the SS medics using human beings as objects, total disregard for basic human values, and torture and death. At the same time, their own survival—like that of de Wind, Micheels, and Cohen—owes much to something that comes through clearly in their accounts: the sense that they had a reason to stay alive, in this case, assisting others. "There were people left in this cruel, hellish world," Micheels observes, "who were truly human, who would risk their lives for someone else."[54] Or as Leo Eitinger, the Norwegian Auschwitz survivor and psychiatrist put it, "it was those people who were capable of showing interest in others who, mentally, had the best chance of retaining their individuality—and perhaps also of surviving as integrated persons."[55] Crucially, Eitinger adds that these were very few. Nevertheless, he later wrote, with special poignancy for this study, that "Physician and nurse prisoners who had been fortunate enough to get positions in Auschwitz where they could maintain their personal norms and values by continuing their prearrest occupation and thus work for and help others had the best chances to survive and to avoid Auschwitz's ethically devastating atmosphere. (Inevitably, though, there were some among the medical personnel who abused their positions for personal gain)."[56]

It is hard to know how much weight should be given to gender in these women's survival. Perhaps the fact that they were women meant that the SS medics responded to their refusal to cooperate differently than if they had been men—but this is speculative. None of these female doctors was a psychoanalyst; although Hautval was a psychiatrist, they do not discuss their survival or that of others in psychoanalytic terms. Yet, none of them seems to have had to "adapt themselves to degradation," which is what Cohen claims was required of all camp inmates. In fact, the opposite seems to be the case, in that they appear to have been able to resist becoming degraded. Bettelheim's arguments seem persuasive on this context, until one recalls that irrespective of their bravery, all of these female doctors survived very largely through luck: each of them recounts moments when they were fortunate not to be executed or otherwise to die of starvation or illness. There is a sense that de Wind's and the others' arguments about "survival through stupor" apply less to these exceptional women than to

---

[54] Micheels, *Doctor #117641*, 76.
[55] Leo Eitinger, *Concentration Camp Survivors in Norway and Israel* (London: Allen and Unwin, 1964), 80, cited in Marcus, *Autonomy in the Extreme Situation*, 179.
[56] Eitinger, "Auschwitz—A Psychological Perspective", 475.

the majority of inmates who did not "enjoy" a morally elevated role in the camp's inmate society. They were among the few whose positions in the camp permitted them to escape David Rousset's claim, put forward in *L'univers concentrationnaire* (1946), that "The camps castrated free minds."[57]

---

[57] David Rousset, *A World Apart*, trans. Yvonne Moyse and Roger Senhouse (London: Secker and Warburg, 1951). "Les camps châtrent les cerveaux libres": *L'univers concentrationnaire* (Paris: Les Éditions de Minuit, 1965 [orig. 1946]), 116.

CHAPTER 4

Revisiting Survival: Hilde O. Bluhm on Early Accounts of the Nazi Concentration Camps

Abstract In 1948, psychoanalyst Hilde O. Bluhm published an article in the *American Journal of Psychotherapy* entitled "How Did They Survive?" Essentially a collective review of 12 books and articles that had been published on the subject up to that point (including Bettelheim, Frankl, and Rousset but also several other now forgotten works by, inter alia, Ernst Wiechert, Rudolf Kalmar, and Georg Karst), Bluhm used the books as a jumping-off point for her own psychoanalytically informed explanation. In this chapter, I pick up on the themes of the first two chapters and reread the same texts in light of the last 80 years of historical research. Bearing in mind de Wind's argument about "survival through stupor," I ask to what extent the authors' accounts have stood the test of time. I do so not to discredit or "unmask" them but to historicize them, asking why certain explanations seem more persuasive than others at different moments in time.

Keywords Holocaust • Survival • Psychological approaches • Postwar period • Estrangement

Primo Levi's story of trying to reach out of a window and pluck an icicle to quench his thirst during the period of his processing into the camp at Auschwitz is one of the most famous incidents in Holocaust literature. Preventing him from taking the icicle, a guard smashes it to the ground; when asked why by Levi, the guard answers: "Here there is no why" (*Hier ist kein warum*). In his now almost unknown memoir of his incarceration in Sachsenhausen from September 1939 to May 1940, published in 1945, Leon Szalet notes a similar event. Informed that he is to be released, Szalet despairs when he is assigned to the "deportation squad," a group of Polish Jews selected to be returned to Poland. Szalet tries to talk to the Stubenältester, in the hope of being taken off the list:

> "Herr Stubenaeltester," I said to him, "I have received word that my release is impending in the immediate future, and I beg you, in view of that, to take me out of the deportation squad."
> Anton looked at me thoughtfully for a few moments and I began to cherish hope—but too soon.
> "Man, don't get any bees in your bonnet. The gentlemen of the Gestapo wouldn't even let a Polish louse crawl out of here, and you think they'll let such a juicy morsel slip through their fingers! And if they want to release you, do you think they'll need a microscope to find you again?"
> "But Herr Stubenaeltester," I protested, "I have ..."
> "But, but! Here there's no buts. You stay in the squad and that's that."[1]

In fact, Szalet and his comrades were lucky on that occasion: the deportation did not take place, for reasons unknown to them. Indeed, Szalet was luckier than just about every other inmate of the camp, for a few days later his release—which hardly anyone in the camp had believed possible— took place, thanks to his daughter Gucia's efforts, and two weeks later they sailed from Genoa to Shanghai. Whether Szalet had a "rich inner life" or a strong sense of attitudinal freedom is not the question; his survival was down to the efforts of his daughter.

In 1948, the American émigré psychoanalyst Hilde O. Bluhm published an article in the *American Journal of Psychotherapy* entitled "How Did They Survive? Mechanisms of Defense in Nazi Concentration Camps." The article is an analysis of 12 articles and books that had been published up until that point on the Nazi camps. These include works that are still

---

[1] Leon Szalet, *Experiment "E": A Report from an Extermination Laboratory*, trans. Catharine Bland Williams (New York: Didier, 1945), 242.

canonical in Holocaust Studies, such as David Rousset's *L'univers concentrationnaire*, as well as early versions of famous texts by Viktor Frankl and Bruno Bettelheim, alongside works that are known today mainly by specialists in the field. The full list, in the editions used by Bluhm, is as follows: Bruno Bettelheim, *My Life in Nazi Concentration Camps* (nd); Karl Billinger, *Fatherland* (1935); Christopher Burney, *The Dungeon Democracy* (1946); Ernst Federn, "Essai sur la psychologie de la terreur," *Syntheses: Revue mensuelle internationale*, 7 and 8 (1946); Viktor Frankl, *Ein Psycholog erlebt das Konzentrationslager* (1946); Rudolf Kalmar, *Zeit ohne Gnade* (1946); George M. Karst, *The Beasts of the Earth* (1942); Benedikt Kautsky, *Teufel und Verdammte* (1946); David Rousset, *The Other Kingdom* (1947); Leon Szalet, *Experiment E* (1945); Seweryna Szmaglewska, *Smoke over Birkenau* (1947); and Ernst Wiechert, *Forest of the Dead* (1947).[2] The review makes no comment about the fact that one of these works was published before the war, others during it, and some after, nor does Bluhm have much to say about the fact that they deal with very different sorts of sites of incarceration, although she does comment on the authors' very varied backgrounds and on the importance of the inmates' "social position" within the camp. Nevertheless, the fact that Bluhm published a review of this sort at the beginning of 1948 is noteworthy and allows us to conduct a scholarly experiment. In this chapter, I reread the texts that Bluhm analyzed for her review article and ask how what she says there has stood the test of time in light of the intervening 80 years' worth of historiography on the Nazi camps and changes in psychoanalytic thought. I do so not to ask what Bluhm got "right" but rather to see how Bluhm's ideas about survival made sense in a particular context and how our ideas today might be different, given how historiography and psychoanalysis have changed over time.

First published in 1948, Bluhm's article was republished as a "classic article" in the *American Journal of Psychotherapy* in 1999. The piece was published in the AJP because it was not a review article in the typical sense; rather, Bluhm's topic was, as she stated, "the mental mechanisms of survival, i.e., the mechanisms of defense developed by the ego in order to

---

[2] I have read the texts in the same version/language that Bluhm did, with the exception of Kautsky, whose book I read in English (*Devils and the Damned*) and Bettelheim, since it is unclear what text she is referring to; the likelihood is that it was an early version of his famous 1943 article, "Individual and Mass Behaviour in Extreme Situations", *Journal of Abnormal and Social Psychology*, 38 (1943), 417–452, which Bettelheim circulated in various forms to friends and colleagues. My thanks to Christian Fleck for advice on this point.

protect the individual from physical death and mental disintegration."³ In her introduction to the 1999 republication, Sophie Freud observed that "it becomes obvious from these books that survival depended to some extent on one's place in the hierarchy and the population group to which one belonged."⁴ As Bluhm writes, following her statement of interest in the question of psychic defense:

> But this prevalence of psychological interest must not make us overlook the great number of other circumstances on which survival in a concentration camp has depended, circumstances which have little to do with mental phenomena of the type mentioned. There was, first of all, the factor of physical stamina: the sick, the old, and the weak were those most likely to perish; there was also the difference in locality and time: in some camps, the food, housing, working, and hygienic conditions were much worse than in others, and it also happened that in the same camp periods of deterioration alternated with periods of improvement! Likewise significant was the kind of work to which the inmate had been assigned: Wiechert, for instance, seems to owe his life to the fact that he was transferred from working in a quarry to mending stockings. Of greatest importance was, furthermore, the official classification of the prisoner. The camp was a rather complicated setup of many divisions and sub-divisions, and every prisoner belonged to several official categories. As far as living conditions were concerned, it made all the difference, whether the internee was a German or a non-German, an "Aryan" or a Jew.⁵

She then notes: "This anarchic power of accident, of the unexpected, of terror, not only ruled over the inmate's life and death in a physical sense, but was perhaps the strongest force in the mental dynamics of concentration camp life."⁶ Here Bluhm anticipates her own article, for she then ends her introduction by stating that: "We are looking for an answer to a socio-psychological problem: *Which were the mental effects produced in a great number of people by an emergency which lasted for years? Did the mass of*

---

³ Hilde O. Bluhm, "How Did They Survive? Mechanisms of Defense in Nazi Concentration Camps", *American Journal of Psychotherapy*, 53:1 (1999), 97. First published in *American Journal of Psychotherapy*, 2:1 (1948), 3–32.
⁴ Sophie Freud, "Commentary: Hilde O. Bluhm, 'How Did They Survive? Mechanisms of Defense in Nazi Concentration Camps'", *American Journal of Psychotherapy*, 53:1 (1999), 124.
⁵ Bluhm, "How Did They Survive?", 97.
⁶ Bluhm, "How Did They Survive?", 98.

prisoners develop typical reactions which were essential for their survival? Of such reactions our books give ample evidence."[7] In other words, Bluhm's starting point is a realistic one: one cannot ask about the psychic mechanisms that contributed to survival without first noting that these mechanisms were by no means the most important factor contributing to survival. But, if the factor of "accident" or "terror" governed the camp and ruled over the inmate's life and death, it must therefore also have had an impact on the inmate's psychic life. It is the latter in which Bluhm is primarily interested.

Beyond the physical conditions for survival, Freud notes, Bluhm turns to what we would regard as a contribution to trauma theory: "She points to a process of depersonalization, a deliberate killing of one's capacity to feel, replacing it with detached observation of self and other, or else absorption in some extraneous task or fantasy. She also comments on the possible lasting after-effects of unintegrated split-off feelings that might then erupt against the wrong person at the wrong moment."[8] Or, in Bluhm's own words: "The protection granted to the individual by the defense mechanism of estrangement was certainly not complete, but without it, many a prisoner who did survive, might have been defeated in his struggle for selfpreservation. In the long run, further modes of physical and psychic adjustment to the camp situation had to be developed."[9] Here Bluhm adumbrates theories later developed by Eitinger, Niederland, de Wind, and others.

What did Bluhm mean by "trauma"? "An incident is called traumatic," Bluhm wrote, "if it subjects the mind to a strong increase in stimulation within a short period of time—with the effect that the stimulation cannot be assimilated or elaborated by normal means."[10] This definition provides an economic model of a protective shield that is broken through, or what Bohleber calls the "too much." It is a model that has become quite commonly known beyond psychoanalysis, thanks to the work of cultural studies and literary scholars, even if some have been criticized for holding too rigid a view of the necessity with which trauma sufferers are condemned to repeat their suffering or for insisting that they have no conscious memory

---

[7] Bluhm, "How Did They Survive?", 99 (emphasis in original).
[8] Freud, "Commentary", 124.
[9] Bluhm, "How Did They Survive?", 106.
[10] Bluhm, "How Did They Survive?", 99.

of the event.[11] What is important about Bluhm's definition in 1948 is that she argues that "exceptionally powerful incidents are likely to have a traumatic effect on everybody," thus turning the analyst's focus to external events.

Freud is impressed that Bluhm utilizes an early form of trauma theory, long before the concept of PTSD had been devised (although as we have seen, other psychologists and psychoanalysts were working towards the same idea at the time). It is a model that can be built on to show how an empathic listener—whether an analyst or an oral history interviewer—can help repair the "communicative dyad between the self and its good object" that has been broken by the trauma, resulting in "absolute inner loneliness and the most extreme hopelessness."[12] But this economic model might also not be satisfactory to describe the full effects of Holocaust-related trauma. What Kahn calls "traumatic desolation" might not be treatable; the trauma, she writes, "is constituted by the very loss of all internal connections, by the disappearance of any possibility of historicization of the experience," meaning that a "black hole left by the traumatic state" has "abolished any hope of gaining a vision of what took place." Kahn argues that only "screen memories" taking the form of sexual and sadistic fantasies, become manifest in analysis; these screen memories should not be understood as the "return of the repressed" or as evidence of some distorted infantile sexuality, but as "'mythical' creations, whose 'narcissistic skin' value is essentially defensive."[13] Furthermore, the long-lasting effects of ongoing persecution such as the Holocaust might manifest in what has been called "cumulative trauma," "sequential trauma," or "persistent trauma," when, in contrast to "ordinary trauma," "a kind of routine and its violent unravelling are constantly intertwined."[14]

[11] See Bohleber, *Destructiveness, Intersubjectivity, and Trauma*, 93, on the economic model of trauma, and Thomas Trezise's comments on Cathy Caruth in *Witnessing Witnessing: On the Reception of Holocaust Survivor Testimony* (New York: Fordham University Press, 2013), 52–53.

[12] Bohleber, *Destructiveness, Intersubjectivity, and Trauma*, 93.

[13] Kahn, *What Nazism Did to Psychoanalysis*, 84–85. See also Dori Laub and Susanna Lee, "Thanatòs and Massive Social Trauma: The Impact of the Death Instinct on Knowing, Remembering, and Forgetting", *Journal of the American Psychoanalytic Association*, 51:2 (2003), 445, for a similar description of screen memories.

[14] Amos Goldberg, *Trauma in First Person: Diary Writing during the Holocaust* (Bloomington: Indiana University Press, 2017), 39, referring to Effi Ziv's concept of "cumulative trauma." See also H. Keilson, "Sequential Traumatization of Children", *Danish Medical Bulletin*, 27:5 (1980), 235–237.

However, in 1948, the question of the patient's ability to historicize trauma lay in the future. Bluhm focused instead on repairing the psychic damage in ways that seemed at the time most promising. It is perhaps no surprise that Freud criticizes Bluhm for what she sees as her main approach to the question of survival, that is, ego-psychology. Freud says that Bluhm's turn to this approach is "not only unfortunate in this context but actually demonstrates the general weakness of that theory." It is worth citing Freud at length here:

> She [Bluhm] worries about the pleasure principle, and characterizes some of the inmates' behavior, such as bedwetting, or lack of cleanliness as "return to the instinctual behavior of early childhood." Yet, I have read of the extreme exhaustion felt by some prisoners, to the point where getting up at night, or earlier than obliged in the morning, to wash in ice cold water, was beyond their strength. This was, however, also a sign that they had given up on survival. The theoretical idea of instinctual regression to infantile bedwetting pleasure adds little to that picture. Her comment that the general lack of sex drive equates regression to the latency period adds to the absurdity of such reasoning. We have fortunately learned in the last fifty years that the breakdown of adult structures is not to be equated with a regression to infancy, even if the behaviors should have somewhat similar appearances.[15]

This seems to be a compelling argument, for as discussed in the introduction, the idea that concentration camp inmates regressed to an infantile state relates to the theory of the identification with the aggressor, a theory to which few analysts any longer subscribe, in this context at least.[16] However, when Freud argues that: "I imagine it is once again her procrustean theoretical framework that prevents the author of seeking one explanation for survival in the qualities of inner strength, endurance, shrewdness, defiance, or even narcissism that seems to have sustained some survivors," the reader is less convinced.[17] Freud is right that Bluhm's theoretical framework, which remained within the bounds of psychoanalytical orthodoxy of the period, prevented her from looking for qualities of inner strength, but 25 years after Freud commented on Bluhm's 1948 article

---

[15] Freud, "Commentary", 124.
[16] Cf. Amos Goldberg's important work on the ways in which Jews in the Warsaw ghetto internalized Nazi views, e.g., when Chaim Kaplan wrote in his diary (25 October 1940) that "We will be like a leper colony, the scum of the human race, *in our own eyes as well.*" Goldberg, *Trauma in First Person*, 191, and the section "The Law and Sadistic Pleasure", 196–199.
[17] Freud, "Commentary", 125.

(actually written in 1947 and published in January 1948), we might take Freud's criticisms and historicize Bluhm's piece differently. What Freud saw as a problem with Bluhm's argument might be regarded as to its credit today in some quarters; not because survivors did not display inner strength, shrewdness, and so on, but because in light of several decades' worth of criticisms of Bettelheim and Frankl, we might feel less confident that those qualities were decisive in distinguishing those who survived from those who did not.

Indeed, in the remainder of this chapter, as I reread the texts analyzed by Bluhm, my focus will primarily be on the question of what Bluhm called "estrangement." This concept echoes de Wind's notion of "stupor," even if Freud is right to highlight the inappropriateness of Bluhm's focus on the pleasure principle or what she saw as a regression to infancy in exhausted camp inmates. Freud's criticisms of ego psychology, which turn on Heinz Hartmann's supposed emphasis on attuning and adapting the ego to reality in a manner akin to an early version of CBT, need not concern us here, but it is important to note that if "estrangement" has analytical value, then it does imply that the ego performs unconscious functions and does not simply follow the id, as Sigmund Freud explained in his later adaptation of his earlier theories in *The Ego and the Id* (1926). That is neither to endorse nor to condemn ego psychology but, from the perspective of history of ideas, to suggest that developments in psychoanalysis had important ramifications for how survival was understood. Although ego psychology has been criticized for taking psychoanalysis beyond its original purview, Hartman, according to Mitchell and Black, paved the way for "new and powerful therapeutic approaches aimed not so much at revealing repressed primitive impulses within the human psyche as at repairing structural dimensions of the psyche itself."[18]

What did Bluhm see as the characteristics of estrangement? She points to three aspects: depersonalization, self-observation, and self-expression, all of which count as "protective blocking mechanisms." In depersonalization, "the ego of the prisoners refused to accept the estrangement it was subjected to," with the result that it "turned the experiences connected

[18] Stephen A. Mitchell and Margaret J. Black, *Freud and Beyond: A History of Modern Psychoanalytic Thought* (New York: Basic Books, 1995), 35. For a view more in line with Freud's, see Ernst Federn, "Psychoanalysis—The Fate of a Science in Exile", in Edward Timms and Naomi Segal (eds.), *Freud in Exile: Psychoanalysis and its Vicissitudes* (New Haven: Yale University Press, 1988), 159, where Federn says that thanks to Hartmann, "psychoanalysis is part of psychiatry" in the US.

with the loss of its feelings into an object of its intellectual interests."[19] This in turn produced the urge to self-observation: "By turning its inner development into an object of investigation, the ego makes the first attempt to restore its contact with the world of objects from which it had withdrawn under the impact of initial trauma."[20] Finally, and crucially, as Bluhm notes, "In the case of our authors," suggesting that this might not always be the case, "the healthy component of self-observation was strengthened by an additional and most essential factor. Luckier than their less articulate comrades, they were privileged by the relieving gift of *self-expression*."[21] Self-observation and self-expression were interrelated, with each generating the other: many of the authors in Bluhm's study attest to a feeling of observing themselves and a desire to write, and vice-versa. "This ability," she asserts, "was a reassurance that the therapeutic component of the 'fever' would predominate over the element of disease."[22]

The factors that come under Bluhm's umbrella concept of "estrangement" are typified by Ernst Wiechert's description of the change that came about him in the camp: "It was the sensation of an ever-growing coldness that spread gradually from deep within until it filled his entire being. It was as if the life he had lived up to now and his whole world were freezing to numbness in this chill. As though he was gazing through a thick sheet of ice at very distant things."[23] Here we see a very clear example of what Bluhm calls "the special mechanisms of defense" developed by the ego to "check the excess of stimulation aroused by the initial experiences."[24] But as with later criticisms of Bettelheim and Frankl, there seems to be little recognition that the "initial experiences" of Sachsenhausen or Buchenwald in 1938, and the subsequent brief incarceration in those camps at that time, might have been different from arriving in Birkenau in 1944.[25]

---

[19] Bluhm, "How Did They Survive?", 102.
[20] Bluhm, "How Did They Survive?", 102.
[21] Bluhm, "How Did They Survive?", 102.
[22] Bluhm, "How Did They Survive?", 103.
[23] Ernst Wiechert, *The Forest of the Dead*, trans. Ursula Stechow (London: Victor Gollancz, 1947), 65.
[24] Bluhm, "How Did They Survive?", 100.
[25] See Kim Wünschmann, "The 'Scientification' of the Concentration Camp: Early Theories of Terror and Their Reception by American Academia", *Leo Baeck Institute Yearbook*, 58 (2013), 111–126, for an excellent discussion.

Indeed, although Frankl's and Bettelheim's writings have given rise to long-running and heated controversies, perhaps Ernst Wiechert is the author among Bluhm's selection who should give us most pause for thought. Little known today outside of Germany, Wiechert was a respected writer and poet in the years before and after World War II. A conservative noted for his passion for the simple, rural life, but also for holding "refined" views about the life of the mind, he was imprisoned in Buchenwald in 1938 for speaking out against the Nazi regime. This sort of complex trajectory suggests that categories commonly used to describe Nazi Germany—perpetrators, victims, and bystanders—need to be approached with caution, since people's views change over time and gray areas exist that do not always allow for clear categorization.[26] On the face of it, this makes his case a clear one of anti-Nazi resistance, meaning that one ought to be able to approach his writings in the same fashion as those of the other authors listed here. Indeed, after the war, one critic regarded his work as offering the most significant encouragement to postwar German literature.[27] However, Wiechert was an author who before 1933 moved in *völkisch* circles and one critic is unhesitating in saying: "that Wiechert stood in a tradition that the National Socialists also built, and that the latter regarded him at the start of their fascist dictatorship not as an enemy but as a writer who absolutely shared their mindset in his writing [*der durchaus in ihrem Sinn schrieb*]."[28] And although *Forest of the Dead* fits the mold of "camp literature" in many respects, it also reads as an account penned by someone too genteel and tender to cope with what was

---

[26] See Raul Hilberg, *Perpetrators, Victims, Bystanders* (London: Secker & Warburg, 1993); Adam Brown, *Judging "Privileged" Jews: Holocaust Ethics, Representation and the "Grey Zone"* (New York: Berghahn Books, 2013); Christina Morina and Krijn Thijs (eds.), *Probing the Limits of Categorization: The Bystander in Holocaust History* (New York: Berghahn Books, 2019); Mary Fulbrook, Stephanie Bird, Stefanie Rauch and Bastiaan Willems (eds.), *Perpetration and Complicity under Nazism and Beyond: Compromised Identities?* (London: Bloomsbury, 2023); Mary Fulbrook, *Bystander Society: Conformity and Complicity in Nazi Germany and the Holocaust* (Oxford: Oxford University Press, 2023).

[27] John R. Frey, "Ernst Wiecherts Werk seit 1945", *The German Quarterly*, 22:1 (1949), 37.

[28] Hattwig, Jörg, *Das Dritte Reich im Werk Ernst Wiecherts: Geschichtsdenken, Selbstverständnis und literarische Praxis* (Frankfurt am Main: Peter Lang, 1984), 12. See also Bill Niven, "Ernst Wiechert and His Role between 1933 and 1945", *New German Studies*, 16 (1990), 1.

happening to him.²⁹ Or, as Bill Niven carefully puts it, *The Forest of the Dead* is a book "not free of a certain chauvinism."³⁰

The book is indeed complex. On the one hand, Wiechert displays a kind of aristocratic regard for independence of thought, virtue, and integrity, which he openly vaunts; this means that a Bettelheim-like emphasis on his "rich inner life" is an obvious truism in his book. The text is written not in the first person but in the third, with the protagonist named Johannes; in Wiechert's own estimation, this maneuver converted lived experience into a higher truth, "that of art."³¹ On the other hand, his book movingly describes his need for the care of comrades in order to facilitate his survival in the camp; most strikingly, he is highly unusual not only in discussing the "asocials" in the camp but in speaking about them in positive terms.

Wiechert's emphasis on self-reliance brings him quite close to de Wind's theory of stupor, or to the theory of estrangement, yet retaining a sense of self-awareness about his behavior:

> He knew best within himself that the sickness of his soul was doing more toward his destruction than could the sickness of his body. Every day he recalled Josef's word: that he must go through this just "like a stone." However, it was not given to him to cast aside all his former life and be a different being from then on. ... Here one could live on only with a "closed door," one could save oneself only if one "saw and heard nothing." Yet Fate had destined him to see and hear all.³²

Indeed, Wiechert's keen sense of observation means he writes of others in the camp with a kindness that is perhaps unexpected. When he writes about the "asocials and criminals," especially, we encounter a very rare description of the "black triangles" that manages not to be riddled with stereotypes. He writes of the asocials' sense of pride and independence,

---

²⁹ See Oskar Seitlin, "Begegnung mit Ernst Wiechert", *The German Quarterly*, 19:4 (1946), 270, who writes: "Zartheit ist vielleicht das Wort, das den Dichter Ernst Wiechert am ehesten beschreibt." Seitlin goes on to claim that Wiechert's physiognomy provides a textbook example of what one expects a poet to look like.

³⁰ Niven, "Ernst Wiechert and His Role between 1933 and 1945", 3.

³¹ Guido Reiner, *Ernst Wiechert im Dritten Reich: Eine Dokumentation* (Paris: Selbstverlag, 1974), 95.

³² Wiechert, *Forest of the Dead*, 104.

irrespective of whether he approves of their (supposed) way of life, and notes:

> However, they had not broken any one of them, not in their souls and not in their bodies. The only thing achieved was that they would now sign anything one gave them for that purpose. Yet, not only had they kept their own philosophy of life, but they had strengthened it, and there was hardly one among them who did not strongly believe in the victory of their cause.[33]

Thus, one sees in Wiechert proof of Bluhm's argument that survival was a matter of those who had the ability to cope with the psychic shock of arrival at the concentration camp and those who did not. "The latter," Bluhm writes, "unable to cope with the threats of the outer world or with their counter-aggressive impulses, 'annihilated' either reality or themselves."[34] As Kalmar put it, "in order to make it through, a robust constitution was important."[35] Or, in Federn's words: "Victorious resistance against the physical and psychical tortures combined was the prerogative of only a few people of strong nature."[36] Later, the psychoanalyst Ilse Grubrich-Simitis observed that "Some of the psychic adaptations which during imprisonment could be regarded as necessary for survival were later often found to have resulted in irreversible structural damage." In other words, the very strategies that had facilitated survival—shutting down one's feelings, "automatization of the ego," as Niederland put it, or simply "robotization," as Joost Meerloo named it—were the sources of illness after the liberation.[37] The "robust constitution" generated its own illnesses:

> The fact that many survivors later had the utmost difficulty in entering into spontaneous empathic relationships was probably due to the persistence of these automatized ego functions, which have been characterized as an armoring of the ego. After all, it would not be surprising to find that survi-

---

[33] Wiechert, *Forest of the Dead*, 112.
[34] Bluhm, "How Did They Survive?", 100.
[35] Rudolf Kalmar, *Zeit ohne Gnade* (Vienna: J&V Edition, n.d. [orig. 1946]), 146.
[36] Ernst Federn, "Essai sur la psychologie de la terreur", *Synthèses: revue mensuelle internationale*, 7–8 (1946), 83.
[37] Grubrich-Simitis, "Extreme Traumatization", 424, and citing Niederland and Meerloo on 423. See also Bernhard Kuschey, *Die Ausnahme des Überlebens. Ernst und Hilde Federn: Eine biographische Studie und eine Analyse der Binnenstrukturen des Konzentrationslagers* (Gießen: Psychosozial Verlag, 2003), vol. 2, 943–944.

vors unconsciously attempt to regulate their vulnerability to overstimulation, especially a repetition of traumatic object loss, by a constant alertness, a readiness to expect the worst, and an avoidance of intense cathexis of new objects.[38]

On the other hand, it is also the case that Wiechert survived because of being transferred to a comfortable indoor job. Bluhm's analysis of his text focuses only on those aspects of it that speak to his psychological ability to survive and ignores just about everything that suggests that his survival was down to luck or the nature of the concentration camp system at that point in time—when few inmates were killed. Nor could Bluhm have written, in 1948, about the long-term consequences of Holocaust trauma, although just a few months after the publication of her article, she would have been able to read Federn's paper in the *Psychiatric Quarterly*, in which he set out clearly the particular fate of the Jews.[39] The result is that her appraisal of survival is, in the end, somewhat pat. In a sense, Bluhm and latter-day analysts are talking past each other: the former is talking about survivors of the early Nazi camps or non-Jewish former inmates who did not experience the worst; the latter tend to focus on the utterly destructive consequences of the Holocaust. No wonder that different accounts of survival compete to be heard. The one exception in Bluhm's readings was Ernst Federn. He described his survival in Buchenwald—and he was there until the end of the war—as a result of his being a political prisoner, and thus "privileged." Although he was a Jew, he had been incarcerated as a "political" and thus was spared the death sentence that was automatically applied to Jews. But Federn primarily regarded his survival as a result of "enormous luck," at least according to his biographer: "The fact that he made life-saving decisions in dangerous moments, i.e., that he was able to react adequately, although he knew the terrible determinants of his reality only to a small extent, and that he received help from friends at the right moment, can probably only be described with the vague term 'luck.'"[40] The article in the Brussels-based journal *Synthèses* (Brussels was where Federn emigrated to after the war) read by Bluhm, however, tends to confirm Bluhm in her opinions: "it was proven again and again that

---

[38] Grubrich-Simitis, "Extreme Traumatization", 425.
[39] Ernst Federn, "Terror as a System: The Concentration Camp", *The Psychiatric Quarterly Supplement*, 22 (1948), 52–86.
[40] Kuschey, *Die Ausnahme des Überlebens*, vol. 2, 946.

morale could, to a large extent, be an effective substitute for a healthy constitution, morale to be understood as the power of the ego to resist all regressive tendencies."[41]

This observation is even clearer when Bluhm turns to discuss the perpetrators' "anal-sadistic practices" that tortured the inmates to the point of insanity. These regressive tendencies were then repeated among the inmates. Among such practices, Bluhm cites a spectrum from "the common system of enforcing strict toilet regulations to monstrous and diabolic tortures." She cites Karst to the effect that inmates could not control themselves and that, because of the cold, "constantly had to let water," and Szalet, who also talks about "bladder sufferers." Bluhm notes too the "anal- and oral-sadistic tendencies of the tormentors," giving Szalet's example of block leaders forcing inmates to drink out of toilets, forcing their heads into the bowls until they were covered with excrement: "At that they almost went out of their minds—that was why their screams had sounded so demented."[42] More bleak still, if that is possible, is Rousset, since he makes such tortures into a kind of concentration camp rule: "Psychologically, losses [i.e., deaths of inmates] were recouped by the sadism which compelled the prisoners to forge the instruments of their own annihilation."[43] As a result of such tortures, Bluhm says, the inmates underwent a form of regression: "In quite a number of cases, the inhibitions of disgust and shame were not strong enough to prevent an individual from a return to childhood reactions, and manifest symptoms of regression occurred."[44] That is to say, although she quite clearly condemns such brutal treatment, Bluhm is unsure to what extent the resulting regression is to be blamed on internal preconditions. We can understand this shortcoming in her analysis as a result of Bluhm's theoretical framework and of the reading she had done for the article—which did not tackle the sort of trauma undergone by Holocaust survivors.

---

[41] Federn, "The Endurance of Torture", in *Witnessing Psychoanalysis*, 48. The chapter is a partial translation of the 1946 essay; for the original, see "Versuch einer Psychologie des Terrors", in Roland Kaufhold (ed.), *Ernst Federn—Versuche zur Psychologie des Terrors. Material zum Leben und Werk von Ernst Federn* (Gießen: Psychosozial Verlag, 1998), 35–75, here 43; "Essai sur la psychologie de la terreur", 84–85. The texts in the three languages differ somewhat.
[42] Bluhm, "How Did They Survive?", 107–108, citing Szalet, *Experiment E*, 42.
[43] Rousset, *A World Apart*, 66.
[44] Bluhm, "How Did They Survive?", 108.

Bluhm's focus on the early camps and her failure to appreciate the degradation of the Holocaust appears even more clearly when she talks about inmates identifying with their aggressor. She notes that "weak egos, which a priori were susceptible to regression, developed reactions particularly characteristic of children." Prominent prisoners—functionaries, kapos, and so on—are the most obvious example of inmates identifying with the oppressors, as a way of trying to free themselves from anxieties: "For losing one's self in a powerful enemy, being 'eaten up' by him, means overcoming one's own helplessness and participating in his omnipotence."[45] Indeed, Bluhm reserves her most strident condemnation for the kapos, citing Kautsky to back up her claims.

This identification with the aggressor represented, according to Bluhm, "the final stage of passive adaptation." It was a paradoxical form of defense, since it meant "survival through surrender"; but, she claims, few inmates resorted to this behavior—a claim that is hard to substantiate with comments like Rousset's that fights took place to try and obtain "privileged" posts.[46] Most inmates, Bluhm goes on, resorted to one form or another of sublimation, by which she means focusing on "pleasant memories of the past, enjoyment of nature, discussions on all kinds of spiritual topics, and sometimes even extraordinary moral accomplishments."[47] The most famous such example, and Bluhm cites it, is Frankl's lecture when he spoke about the meaning of life; relieving the other inmates from their desperate mood, they afterwards "thanked him with tears in their eyes."[48] She notes, however, that religion, at least in the authors she analyses, fared poorly and did not provide the sort of consolation to the inmates that one might expect. Even the religious Wiechert could not maintain his faith in a God who had allowed this to happen. By contrast, political affiliation, and being able to maintain it in the camp, proved a source of strength. Such claims can certainly be backed up by the texts, although we might bear in mind that these are exceptions rather than rules—what Primo Levi called "moments of reprieve."[49] More normal was the description offered by Herbert Bloch, one of the first Americans to enter several concentration camps and a senior figure in the civilian affairs administration, in his assess-

---

[45] Bluhm, "How Did They Survive?", 115.
[46] Rousset. *A World Apart*, 84–85.
[47] Bluhm, "How Did They Survive?", 116.
[48] Bluhm, "How Did They Survive?", 117.
[49] See for example Rousset, *A World Apart*, ch16.

ment of a women's slave labor camp in Lenzing, Austria, published shortly before Bluhm's:

> The entire life structure and community outlook are pervaded with a morbid sense of insecurity and intense fear. Life is reduced to anarchy, kept in check only by the firmest discipline. Behavior is reduced to survival activities. The records display a constant morbid preoccupation with the destruction of the family and isolation from the rest of the world. There is strong evidence of traumatic shock, excessive apathy, an intense desire for survival, profound insecurity, and fear.[50]

Here we might detect a gendered assessment: even if all the inmates are fixated on survival, the women are absorbed with the fate of their families, the men with identifying with the guards. Several decades of historiography would suggest that this distinction does not hold, even if the general picture is still that women were more likely to engage in mutual aid in the camps than were men.[51] The picture becomes much more complicated when we include inmates such as "asocials," who tended to be excluded from most literature (Wiechert is exceptional in that regard), and we see that gender is but one, albeit an important variable. It is nevertheless clear that Rousset was right when he stressed how extraordinary it was to see inmates who remained steadfast and "who preserved their dignity intact until the very end."[52]

This complexity is evident in Burney's book, which might be why Bluhm has little to say about it. Burney's *Dungeon Democracy* was one of seven books reviewed by Norbert Guterman in *Commentary* in July 1946. The review (which also included Szalet's *Experiment E*) is nothing like as interesting as Bluhm's, providing little more than summaries of the books, but Guterman's comments about Burney are suggestive. Noting that Burney claims that the majority of inmates imitated the behavior of the guards rather than seeking to create a united front, and that he concludes as a result "that continental Europe holds little prospect of evolving a democratic way of life," Guterman goes on:

---

[50] Herbert A. Bloch, "The Personality of Inmates of Concentration Camps", *American Journal of Sociology*, 52:4 (1947), 336. Lenzing was a sub-camp of Mauthausen.

[51] See e.g., Sarah Held, *If This is a Woman. Inside Ravensbrück: Hitler's Concentration Camp for Women* (London: Little, Brown, 2015); Zoë Waxman, *Women in the Holocaust: A Feminist History* (Oxford: Oxford University Press, 2017).

[52] Rousset, *A World Apart*, 96.

While these theoretical views are highly disputable and seem in part influenced by the author's belief in the moral superiority of the British, his book is extremely valuable as a picture of the psychological degradation of the camp inmate, which corroborates and supplements the well-known analyses of Dr. Bruno Bettelheim. It also contains an excellent account of the mechanism by which this effect was achieved. The SS troops ruled the camp by proxy, that is, they charged certain groups of prisoners with the responsibility of keeping order; these privileged groups in turn granted responsibilities and privileges to others, and as a result a caste system arose in which those who were most ruthless had the greatest chances for survival. Christopher Burney believes that many lives could have been saved if the prisoners had displayed greater moral strength and solidarity. Of all the prisoners, only the Jews were not given even this opportunity—pariahs among pariahs, they were doomed to die no matter what they did.[53]

Perhaps one reason why Bluhm hardly mentions Burney's text is that it is the one that deals most explicitly with the murder of the Jews (Rousset and others mention but do not deal at length with the Holocaust). Perhaps she regarded the genocide of the Jews—insofar as she knew about it at all—as merely another confirmation of the importance of identification with the aggressor. In fact, the richest, most detailed texts in Bluhm's review article—those by Burney, Rousset, Kautsky, and Szmaglewska—are those which receive the least detailed attention by her. In some ways this is to be expected: we are talking about a review article of a dozen works, after all, one which focuses on a particular psychological problem and not an in-depth textual analysis of each work. Yet one cannot help but notice that these texts are more complex than Bluhm allows. In the books by those former inmates who had long experience of the camps—in fact, who were held in them until the end of the war—we encounter versions of survival that, even if not explicitly set out in psychological terms, problematize Bluhm's arguments.

When discussing the conditions with which inmates had to cope, for example, Szmaglewska left no room for wishful thinking. "The prisoner must therefore take care of himself and provide for his own rights," she writes at one point; "The catchword 'live while you may' seizes many," she states at another.[54] Szmaglewska's book is notable for many reasons, not

---

[53] Norbert Guterman, "Seven Books on Nazi Atrocities", *Commentary* (July 1946).

[54] Seweryna Szmaglewska, *Smoke over Birkenau*, trans. Jadwiga Rynas (Warsaw: Książka i Wiedza/Auschwitz-Birkenau State Museum, 2001), 318, 250.

least for being among the very first accounts of Auschwitz to have been published after the war. Given how little time Szmaglewska had to gather her thoughts, it is also remarkably insightful where adaptation to camp life is concerned:

> This stripping off the clothes and cutting the hair of a man entering the camp are essential symbols. Man is left naked and deprived of his buckler. He must create in himself a new relation to reality, the basis of which must be his inner integrity. Some souls stand erect, like chestnut flowers when the husks protecting them have fallen off. There are others who, like an amoeba, dissolve in the general moral chaos of the camp, adjusting their shape to the pressure from without.
>
> There are atavisms and instincts long asleep which, though not extinguished, would remain dormant through many years of life. But the abnormal existence in a concentration camp wakens those instincts and calls them to life. The eternal white and black, the eternal good and evil rise within the human being and come to the surface.[55]

This is a complex passage, for although it refers to the need for "inner integrity," it also suggests that some who survived did so by being like amoeba, shape shifting according to the general requirements, bending to the will of the majority. And when she refers to the "eternal good and evil" rising to the surface, it is unclear what Szmaglewska means. Does she mean in a positive way, in that people are able to judge what is right and wrong, or does she mean that notions of good and evil are flexible in ways that allow one to survive in circumstances of, as she puts it, abnormality? Either way, this is not a text that unequivocally supports Bluhm's arguments about regression or identification with the aggressor, or about the need for a rich inner life in order to survive.

Bluhm notes that Kautsky refers to the classification of inmates, with a focus on the kapos; she notes too that he comments on the high incidence of insanity and/or suicide among new inmates in the first days after entering the camp; that he accounts for the disappearance of the sexual drive as a result not of malnutrition but of "mental pressure", and that inmates became insensible to physical injury and "normal" illnesses such as colds. She interprets Kautsky's comments about cleanliness and order as revealing of the Nazis' anal-sadistic tendencies. But most strikingly, Bluhm ends her article by appealing to Kautsky's sense of optimism: "He feels by no

---

[55] Szmaglewska, *Smoke over Birkenau*, 250–251.

means pessimistic about mankind, having observed that even under the most horrible conditions of the concentration camp, compassion, friendship, and humaneness were not completely absent. He holds that the destructive forces in society can be mastered, once social and political achievements will have freed man from want and fear."[56] It is true that the final section of Kautsky's book, on the liberation of Buchenwald, concludes with a rousing celebration of international anti-fascist solidarity. Nevertheless, the sections on Auschwitz—and even a well-informed paragraph on Treblinka—reveal a much darker story.

All of this said, Bluhm's review deals with texts by authors who had been inmates of Nazi concentration camps for greater or lesser periods of time. They had not been victims of the Holocaust qua genocide of the Jews, a point that is worth stressing for the sole reason that non-Jews witnessed and were victims of unbridled cruelty in the camps, they had to cope with random violence and the permanent fear of unpredictability, but they were not slated for murder in ways that Jews were. Thus, their survival was possible in ways that was not the case for Jews, for whom survival was exceptional. The cases of Frankl and Bettelheim are unusual in that, although today we would probably classify them as Holocaust survivors, they saw the inside of Nazi concentration camps at a point in time when Jews as such were not being sent to camps and when release was the likely outcome—as indeed it was for both of them. Arguments about stupor or a rich inner life seem less germane to the place of the Jews in the camps later in the war, even those, like de Wind, who held "privileged" positions. What Holocaust survivors often articulated after the war was something altogether different—a sense of death in life.

For example, one of Greenspan's interviewees discussed at length his sense of estrangement after the war brough about by the feeling that, although still alive, in some sense he had died during the Holocaust. "Yet, as Leon emphasizes, this capacity not to feel, not to think, not to identify or empathize, was equally required for survival and also a result of the 'realistic assessment' of the world."[57] If our understanding of "estrangement" differs now from Bluhm's, it is because Bluhm tried to make sense of the accounts she reviewed using the concepts of her profession at that time. As Robert Krell somewhat scathingly noted:

[56] Bluhm, "How Did They Survive?", 121.
[57] Greenspan, *On Listening to Holocaust Survivors*, 64.

Bluhm posed the question: "Which were the mental effects produced in a great number of people by an emergency which lasted for years? Did the mass of prisoners develop typical reactions which were essential for their survival?" She noted the use of "emotional frigidity," a state akin to depersonalization; self-observation and self-expression (in mind only); as well as attempts to maintain a sense of cleanliness in a world of filth. Her article consists of an examination of the written works of survivors. In an effort to explain some of the horrors, she discussed weak egos, regression to childhood, and identification with the aggressor. Unfortunately, no attempt is made to examine the possibility that the unimaginable horrors caused reactions not explainable through existing theories.[58]

This seems to me a little unfair. Certainly, Bluhm made use of the concepts of her time (regression, the ego giving itself up, and so on), yet her explanation of the workings of trauma—focusing on its "density" (i.e., "the amount of excitation it arouses within a short unit of time") and on its "degree of unexpectedness," provides a strong sense of how what happened was, as she puts it, "beyond expectation"—and when Bluhm uses that phrase she is referring to Jews and active anti-Nazis who were "mentally prepared for their deportation" but still were shocked by the arrival at the camp.[59] Under the "anarchic rule of accident," inmates were constantly unable to adjust: "The prisoner never knew what would happen to him in the next minute. Although ill treatment, or torture, or death, were expected constantly,—in most instances they did occur unexpectedly. The individual was always prepared, and—was never prepared."[60] Under such conditions, the ego could not restore its normal method of functioning, which "made it retain its protective 'coat of ice.'"[61] Bluhm is both trenchant and insightful with respect to the authors she surveys, and way off the mark when it comes to the assessment of Holocaust survivors who passed through Auschwitz, Majdanek, Gross-Rosen, the slave labor subcamps, the death marches, and the horrors of the concentration camps in the last months of the war, or who spent the war years in hiding or passing as Aryan. In other words, Bluhm's analysis is appropriate for understanding survival and its consequences in the concentration camps in the strict sense; most analyses of Holocaust trauma today focus on survivors of the

[58] Krell, "Psychiatry and the Holocaust", 9–10.
[59] Bluhm, "How Did They Survive?", 105.
[60] Bluhm, "How Did They Survive?", 105.
[61] Bluhm, "How Did They Survive?", 105.

death camps and the broader "apparatus" of the Holocaust. The sort of psychotic survivors studied by Laub, for example, do not feature in Bluhm's work.[62]

In what sounds like a well-considered paragraph, Bluhm actually, as Freud observed, fails adequately to imagine the circumstances of the concentration camp:

> All these considerations are based on the assumption that mental illness can, in principle, be induced by exogenic causes. We are well aware that this is only half the truth, and that external factors do not become effective unless their influence is warranted by individual predisposition. However, few people would become ill only on account of their predisposition, were it not for the additional injurious experiences to which life has exposed them.[63]

In this curiously disembodied, agentless statement, we see the other side of the coin from the sort of statements that justified rejecting compensation claims in the decades after Bluhm's article was published. Where Bluhm argued that "injurious experiences" brought to light existing "predispositions," the analysts of the compensation claims placed the emphasis on the predispositions, playing down the external effects. In both cases, there was a failure—whether deliberate or not—to make the imaginative and theoretical leap required to understand the enormity of what had happened in the concentration camps and death camps. In the case of the compensation claim assessors, this was a conscious strategy; in Bluhm's case, it was a misperception born from reading accounts of the camps that did not deal with the sorts of experiences that Holocaust survivors were detailing in their compensation claims.

This failure should not be condemned in an off-hand way; it is clear to us now, after decades worth of clinical and theoretical work on trauma/PTSD. As Henry Greenspan notes of his own training with Henry Krystal, himself an Auschwitz survivor: "Trauma's extension to signify virtually every anguish that survivors endure—and, much more broadly, to stand for historical 'catastrophe' in general—would have been barely

---

[62] Dori Laub, "From Speechlessness to Narrative: The Case of Holocaust Historians and of Psychiatrically Hospitalized Survivors", *Literature and Medicine*, 24:2 (2005), 253–265. But see Hilel Klein, "Problems in the Psychotherapeutic Treatment of Israeli Survivors of the Holocaust", in Krystal (ed.), *Massive Psychic Trauma*, 233–244, which predates Laub's study by many years.

[63] Bluhm, "How Did They Survive?", 109.

conceivable in those earlier days."[64] And it is also clear thanks to the intervening decades worth of historiography. Bluhm's article recapitulates a familiar theme in historical writing on the Holocaust, that aligns the murder of the Jews with the concentration camp system. As recent work shows, camps such as Dachau, Buchenwald, and Sachsenhausen had nothing to do with the Holocaust, qua murder of the Jews, until late in the war when they became dumping grounds for Jews who had been forcibly evacuated from camps further east, in the wake of the Red Army's westward advance. This is why there were large numbers of Jews in the camps in the Reich proper, with Belsen being the prime example—a camp that held small number of Jews as "privileged" inmates, that is, those who could be used by the Nazis for prisoner swaps or other forms of diplomatic negotiation, suddenly became one of the worst of the Holocaust-related camps at the start of 1945 as tens of thousands of dying Jews were dumped there in appalling conditions. Apart from the training of camp guards at Dachau and the brief moment in late 1938/early 1939 following the November pogrom when some 30,000 Jewish men were incarcerated, the concentration camps under the control of the SS's Inspectorate of Concentration Camps (IKL) had little to do with the genocide of the Jews.[65] Nevertheless, this confusion between concentration camps and the Holocaust is still very much in evidence in popular understanding of the Nazi crimes, so we should hardly be shocked at Bluhm's lack of clarity on this point in 1948.

More important is the fact that Bluhm read these texts with her psychological research question in mind. As a result, we might now consider that whatever insights her article provides, she missed a great deal of other relevant information. First, from today's perspective, merely the fact that these texts appeared either contemporaneously with or so soon after the demise of the institutions they described is noteworthy; historians are still uncovering the extent of the early literature on the Third Reich and its crimes, and the ways in which different disciplines did or did not respond to them. In that respect, despite the criticisms of some of its members

[64] Henry Greenspan, "Introduction" to Greenspan et al., "Engaging Survivors: Assessing 'Testimony' and 'Trauma' as Foundational Concepts", *Dapim—Studies on the Holocaust*, 28:3 (2014), 190.
[65] See, for example, Jane Caplan and Nikolaus Wachsmann (eds.), *Concentration Camps in Nazi Germany: The New Histories* (London: Routledge, 2010); Nikolaus Wachsmann, *KL: A History of the Nazi Concentration Camps* (London: Little, Brown, 2015); Dan Stone, *The Holocaust: An Unfinished History* (London: Pelican, 2023).

today, psychoanalysis was by no means the slowest of the disciplines to tackle the problem of Nazism. Bluhm had to read between the lines to discern "psychological" themes in her work, in the texts penned by most of these authors (with exceptions of course in Bettelheim, Federn, and Frankl), and disregarded many other issues. For example, she notes that Kautsky's book is "actually a comprehensive sociology of the concentration camp," although that is not what interested her.[66]

Many other topics evident in these books were not noticed by Bluhm. Today we might stress topics such as gender, the family, sexuality, the history of emotions or an experiential history, the "gray zone," the relations between different agencies within the camp administration, the camps' interactions with the surrounding environment, the camps' role in the Holocaust, and so on. Recent scholarly work has addressed the issue of language and translation in the camps, the extent to which the Nazi camps provide the "ideal type" of the concentration camp phenomenon, the trials of kapos in Israel and elsewhere, and the creation of postwar survivor associations, and the exclusion of "asocials" from those associations and from compensation packages, among many other topics.[67] For some decades from the 1960s onwards, particularly following the Eichmann trial and Frankfurt Auschwitz trials, the historiography focused on the institutional history of the Nazi camps and the role in creating a society governed by terror; in more recent years—notably, as those who were young during the Third Reich have aged—that image has given way to that of a society characterized by "consensus," in which the bulk of the population groomed itself to become Nazified even as Nazi ideological measures were imposed from above. That is by no means a unanimous view, but whichever position a historian takes, the place of the concentra-

[66] Bluhm, "How Did They Survive?", 97.
[67] For example: Emma Kuby, *Political Survivors: The Resistance, the Cold War, and the Fight against Concentration Camps after 1945* (Ithaca: Cornell University Press, 2019); Maximilian Becker, "International Resistance Veterans' Organisations in the Debate on Limitation in 1965", in Suzanne Bardgett, Christine Schmidt and Dan Stone (eds.), *Beyond Camps and Forced Labour* (Cham: Palgrave Macmillan, 2020), 231–252; Dan Porat, *Bitter Reckoning: Israel Tries Holocaust Survivors as Nazi Collaborators* (Cambridge, MA: The Belknap Press of Harvard University Press, 2019); Michaela Wolf (ed.), *Interpreting in Nazi Concentration Camps* (London: Bloomsbury, 2016); Susanne zur Nieden, *Unwürdige Opfer: Die Aberkennung von NS-Verfolgten in Berlin 1945 bis 1949* (Berlin: Metropol, 2003); Henning Borggräfe, *Zwangsarbeiterentschädigung: Vom Streit um "vergessene Opfer" zur Selbstaussöhnung der Deutschen* (Göttingen: Wallstein, 2014); Jacob Flaws, *Spaces of Treblinka: Retracing a Death Camp* (Lincoln: University of Nebraska Press, 2024).

tion camps in the Third Reich is crucial. We should of course not admonish Bluhm for not tackling these issues in her article; to the contrary, hers is one of the earliest scholarly pieces of writing after the war to set out just how important the camps were. That she did not understand them in quite the same way that we might do today is not a criticism; it in fact is a tribute to work like hers, written immediately after the war, insofar as it set research agendas that have remained in place ever since.

Bluhm's interpretation, in other words, needs to be historicized, for then we can understand the limitations of her approach. Not many years later, analysts would face the truth that many survivors had been unable to "rebuild their egos" in the way described by Bluhm. Her argument about estrangement unquestionably holds water for some survivors, as we have already seen in the previous two chapters. But it fails to capture the traumatic experience of the Holocaust that most survivors underwent. What Greenspan and others have shown is that perfectly healthy people became ill after the Holocaust, meaning that psychologists no longer believe that psychological illnesses relate solely to suppressed problems of childhood but are triggered by events later in life. Greenspan's approach—to hold conversations with survivors over many years, rather than to interview them once for a project—shows how as the survivors aged, as they changed over time, and as their children and grandchildren dealt with the Holocaust's legacy, so these changes were mirrored in a more sophisticated historiography that could distinguish between different sorts of victims of Nazi persecution and explain how the camps changed over time. Individual survivors have often existed since the end of the war as "lived contradictions," embodying "death in life" one moment, and surprising resilience the next. Today, debate is more about how to define trauma, to what extent traumatic symptoms are heightened by particular types of events, and how long patients will suffer, rather than whether victims of the Holocaust reverted to childhood or identified with their aggressors. Nevertheless, given the ways in which survivors are heroized, Greenspan's warnings that they are just ordinary people who need love and care in the same way as everyone does, is not always in evidence.

Bluhm argued that survivors who chose to write about their concentration camp experiences were taking steps to recovery. By tackling the subject, they "turned toward that very reality which had threatened to overpower them; and they rendered this reality into an object of their 'creation.'" The writing is then a form of auto-therapy in which the survivor begins to take repossession of psychic health: "This turn from a passive suffering to an active undertaking indicated that the ego was regaining control. The association between self-observation and self-expression became a most successful mechanism of survival."[68] But she wrote without full appreciation of the horror of the Holocaust—most of the works included in her review dealt with the concentration camps at an earlier stage of their development when they had nothing to do with the genocide of the Jews—and with little appreciation that the idea of inmates having "protective blocking mechanisms" hardly held up in the face of the extremes that were to follow. The mass murder of the Jews was of course known about when Buhm was writing: many newsreels, radio and press reports, exhibitions and publications had already appeared. But the books and articles that Bluhm surveyed, even when they were about or partly about Auschwitz (Szmaglewska, Kautsky), were written by former inmates whose trajectories meant that they had not been persecuted as Jews and/ or had had little personal contact with the Holocaust. Her article simply could not appreciate the depth of the trauma suffered by Holocaust victims. Stories that have become familiar to us of ghettos, death camps, death marches, the horrific conditions in the camps at the end of the war, and the discovery of the destruction of one's family and community do not feature in Bluhm's account; as a result, her emphasis on protective blocking mechanisms speaks, in the context of the Holocaust, to those like de Wind or the female inmate physicians of Block 10 who retained some sense of being able to make autonomous decisions and who benefited from meaningful relationships with others in the camp. For most victims of the Holocaust, even her concept of "estrangement" does not capture what it meant to survive.

---

[68] Bluhm, "How Did They Survive?", 103.

CHAPTER 5

Conclusion

Abstract Reflecting on the intersections of historiography and psychoanalysis as set out in the previous chapters, I show that each discipline needs to be historicized but that when juxtaposed, they offer a vocabulary, an analytical approach, and a style of approaching past action that can provide powerful explanations for phenomena that appear to exceed the limits of rational assessment. Confronted with the massive trauma of Nazism and the Holocaust, some psychoanalysts argued that their discipline had nothing to offer; others suggested that analysis could in some cases be used but only with great care. Similarly, historians debated whether their inherently empirical and rational discipline had the tools to explain the Holocaust. Although there will never be a completely satisfactory explanation, I argue here that employing psychoanalytic terms helps in grappling with the monstrosity of the Nazi crimes and their effects on the Nazis' victims.

Keywords Anti-Semitism • Psychoanalysis • Holocaust historiography

According to Martin Bergmann, evidence from clinical practice:

> suggests that only few survivors and not many children of survivors could tolerate the rigors of the classical psychoanalytic technique, particularly the anonymity of the therapist. This should not be interpreted to mean that they all fall diagnostically into the borderline psychotic category, but the Holocaust trauma has adversely affected the structure of the ego. One might say in general that the Holocaust trauma was a trauma to the superego, ego, and id. The fact that the camps were instituted by a government representing parental authority offended the superego. That the cruelty witnessed went beyond ordinary wishes of the id shook both the id and the ego.[1]

Bergmann's claim, from the early 1980s, rings true insofar as many children of survivors have reported growing up with psychological disturbances. On the other hand, there is considerable contradictory evidence to the effect that survivors and their children age with resilience and are no more susceptible to psychological illnesses than anyone else. That topic is, however, beyond the scope of this short book, and pertains to debates around the advantages and limitations of the concept of "survivor syndrome."

Along the same lines as Bergmann's statement, there is evidence to support contrary views of psychoanalysts: that after the war they resisted bringing the Holocaust into their patients' or their own analyses or that they were among the first to ask what the genocide of the Jews meant for their profession and vice versa: what psychoanalysis could provide as a resource for understanding it. Emily Kuriloff's claims about émigré analysts shutting their persecution off from their conscious minds certainly seems to hold true for those she examines, who emigrated from Nazi Europe before the war. In the context of Israel, Judith Stern talks about the "collusion of silence" between psychiatrists, psychotherapists, society at large, and Holocaust survivors, saying that this collusion "now looks like a distortion of history and of the inner world of the patients."[2] But the survivor analysts such as de Wind, Cohen, and Micheels to some extent tell a different story, in which their practice was informed by their

---

[1] Martin S. Bergmann, "Recurrent Problems in the Treatment of Survivors and Their Children", in Martin S. Bergmann and Milton E. Jucovy (eds.), *Generations of the Holocaust* (New York: Columbia University Press, 1990), 265.

[2] Judith Stern, "The Eichmann Trial and its Influence on Psychiatry and Psychology", *Theoretical Inquiries in Law*, 1:2 (2000), 402.

survival—albeit the conclusions they drew from their therapeutic practice seem to contradict their accounts of their own survival. The female doctors who survived Block 10 certainly felt able to discuss their experiences, and as Hilde Bluhm's 1948 article shows, a steady flow of books about the Nazi camps was being published from before the end of the war, and these works were of interest to psychoanalysts.

In 1940, Otto Fenichel began an article on the psychoanalysis of anti-Semitism with the words: "Please do not expect too much from me. Antisemitism is a very complicated phenomenon."[3] Just a few years after the end of World War II, the Yale psychoanalyst Rudolph M. Loewenstein noted that what we would now call the Holocaust had not ended anti-Semitism:

> Long before the end of World War Two it was easy to foresee that the defeat of Nazi Germany would not put an end to anti-Semitism. On the contrary, it could be expected to continue both in Europe and America. For the Nazis had replenished the store of historical causes that form the permanent stockpile of anti-Semitism. They had broadcast lies which, however fantastic, had obtained credence and would continue to have repercussions throughout the world. They had demonstrated that it was relatively easy to persecute Jews, and even to exterminate them, with impunity. And above all they left in the wake of their defeat an impoverished, ravaged, ruined, weakened Europe; a Europe more deeply torn politically than perhaps ever before in her history.[4]

For all the criticisms of Loewenstein's book—its too ready acceptance of stereotypes about Jews, for example—this passage remains insightful. One can quibble with the idea that anti-Semitism is as widespread and threatening as some commentators claim, but that it still exists and that it continues to give rise to scandals and debate is undeniable. One of the recurring tropes of survivor testimony, from the immediate postwar period until today, is sadness and shock at the fact that the Holocaust did not see the demise of anti-Semitism. Over 30 years ago, Eric Santner

---

[3] Otto Fenichel, "Psychoanalysis of Antisemitism", *American Imago*, 1:2 (1940), 24. The text was originally a lecture delivered in Prague in April 1937. On Fenichel as an émigré, see Kuriloff, *Contemporary Psychoanalysis and the Legacy of the Third Reich*, 7–8. And for more on the 1940 article, see Frosh, *Antisemitism and Racism*, 29.

[4] Loewenstein, *Christians and Jews*, 200. For a similar argument, that sees antisemitism as "a sort of sociopathology", see J. F. Brown, "Social and Psychological Factors in the Anti-Semitic Attitude", *The Journal of Educational Sociology*, 16:6 (1943), 351–354.

observed that: "Where the Jews were once blamed for the traumas of modernity, the Holocaust now seems to figure as the irritating signifier of the traumas and disorientations of postmodernity." With specific reference to film, he goes on: "Whereas once it was the Jews, now the Shoah itself serves as a screen on which is projected, as something that intervenes from the outside—from Asia—that which ultimately keeps Germans from feeling continuous with themselves."[5] Although there have been many Holocaust-related scandals and although German memory politics and culture has shifted considerably since 1990, it is hard to deny, in light of the rise of the AfD and, in a more rarified milieu, the debates over German colonialism, boycotting Israel, and Holocaust memory, that Santner's insight is compelling.

That sadness, however, needs to be tempered by awareness of one's own subject position. Dominick LaCapra warns against the denial of affect, or transference, in research, as well as against over-identification with the object of research. One could argue that contemporary fears about a resurgence of anti-Semitism are after-effects of the Holocaust insofar as Jews in North America and most of Europe, who live lives less molested than at any point in Jewish history, feel threatened in ways that suggest an inability to work through a traumatic family and community past. LaCapra sensitively offers a way forward: "not to dwell obsessively on trauma as an unclaimed experience that occasions the paradoxical witnessing of the breakdown of witnessing but rather to elaborate a mutually informative, critically questioning relation between memory and reconstruction that keeps one sensitive to the problematics of trauma."[6]

At the same time, LaCapra is one of the few historians who values psychoanalytic vocabulary and insights for understanding history.[7] He does not deny the significance of the rational, bureaucratic aspects of the Final Solution, such as the railway timetables emphasized by Raul Hilberg. But

---

[5] Eric L. Santner, *Stranded Objects: Mourning, Memory, and Film in Postwar Germany* (Ithaca: Cornell University Press, 1990), 51, 52.

[6] Dominick LaCapra, *History and Memory after Auschwitz* (Ithaca: Cornell University Press, 1998), 183. See also LaCapra, "Reflections on Trauma, Absence, and Loss", in Peter Brooks and Alex Woloch (eds.), *Whose Freud? The Place of Psychoanalysis in Contemporary Culture* (New Haven: Yale University Press, 2000), 178–204. See also Michael Roper, "Analysing the Analysed: Transference and Counter-Transference in the Oral History Encounter", *Oral History*, 31:2 (2003), 20–32.

[7] See also Kahn, *What Nazism Did to Psychoanalysis*, 122–123.

he believes—rightly, in my opinion—that there is more to say: "there is also a sense in which the brutality, cruelty, and elation involved in acts of perpetrators are not entirely explained by the bureaucratic or technological imperative. The bureaucrat's relation to a cold and vicious 'superego' involving literal or figurative distance from the dehumanized, debased other may well be one component in a larger, tangled constellation of forces."[8] In a very dense passage, LaCapra sets out what he believes these different forces consisted of: "certain aspects of Nazi behaviour and motivation can only be understood, however partially and with no pretence to full explanation of the Shoah, by seeing them in terms of anxieties about ritual contamination and the desire to seek purification through a displaced, disoriented mode of sacrificialism and victimization, involving at times a redemptive quest, a negative sublime, and carnivalesque elements." These forces acquire their significance precisely because they are "inserted within a modern, industrialized, bureaucratized context where they seem utterly uncanny and out of place."[9]

LaCapra offers a powerful way of understanding the Holocaust, one that owes a great deal to psychoanalysis. His approach is aimed at understanding the perpetrators, however, not the survival of the victims. There is nothing wrong with that, of course—indeed, it seems strange that there are not more attempts to approach the perpetrators in this way, given that their actions exceed the bounds of cost-benefit, instrumental-rational calculation. Earlier attempts to do so, such as Henry Dicks' book *Licensed Mass Murder* (1972) and the other publications of the Columbus Centre, have been largely forgotten.[10] What is missing in LaCapra's account—and this is remarkable, given its significance to the origins of psychoanalysis—is any discussion of sexuality. In fact, perhaps the best recent account of the sexual aspects of Nazism is Jonathan Littell's novel *The Kindly Ones*, although its emphasis on its protagonist's sexual perversity tends (deliberately, perhaps, as a means of brutalizing the reader) to reproduce the thing

---

[8] LaCapra, *History and Memory after Auschwitz*, 190.
[9] LaCapra, *History and Memory after Auschwitz*, 191.
[10] Henry V. Dicks, *Licensed Mass Murder: A Socio-Psychological Study of Some SS Killers* (London: Chatto Heinemann for Sussex University Press, 1972). See Danae Karydaki, *History and Psychoanalysis in the Columbus Centre: The Meaning of Evil* (London: Routledge, 2023).

it is ostensibly critiquing.[11] It seems that scholars today are wary of addressing the topic of Nazism's erotic appeal, leaving the field open to sensationalists. Suggestive guides to how to approach it can be found, however, in Karl Kraus and in some other contemporaries' writings, such as the controversial Erich Fromm and Wilhelm Reich. Historians such as George Mosse, Jane Caplan, and Dagmar Herzog have also addressed the topic, but it remains a difficult one. Although the theme of sexual violence during the Holocaust is one that can now be openly discussed—albeit historians tend to ask women questions about sexual violence, forgetting that women are not only to be defined through their sexuality—the erotic dimension of prejudice and perpetration remains a sensitive issue. Where the relationship between sex and the Holocaust has been addressed, historians tend to veer away from the sort of explanations offered by psychoanalysis, not because, as Elizabeth Heinemann says, historians are "too conservative" to consider sexuality but "because of epistemological differences among disciplines."[12] We need what Susannah Heschel, following queer theorist Elizabeth Freeman, calls an "erotohistoriography" that provides "a logic to the illogic of antisemitic eruptions and the gratification they offer."[13] By this, I do not so much mean a study of historians' carnal relationship to the past (which is part of what Freeman calls for) as an analysis of the libidinal and erotic drives that shaped the way people in the past behaved, especially when trying to understand the appeal of fascism in general and Nazism in particular and, in some cases, the ways in which their victims responded.[14]

---

[11] One might make the same point about Martin Amis' *The Zone of Interest*, although Paul Doll, the camp commandant in the novel, represents a more normative toxic masculinity, as is clear from his repeated insistence that he is "normal." Earlier examples include Klaus Theweleit's *Male Fantasies*, D. M. Thomas's *The White Hotel* and Liliana Cavani's 1974 film, *The Night Porter*.

[12] Elizabeth D. Heinemann, "Sexuality and Nazism: The Doubly Unspeakable", in Dagmar Herzog (ed.), *Sexuality and German Fascism* (New York: Berghahn Books, 2005), 27–28.

[13] Susannah Heschel, "Erotohistoriography: Sensory and Emotional Dimensions of Antisemitism", in Scott Ury and Guy Miron (eds.), *Antisemitism and the Politics of History* (Waltham, MA: Brandeis University Press, 2023), 67. More broadly, see Todd McGowan, *The Racist Fantasy: Unconscious Roots of Hatred* (London: Bloomsbury, 2022) and Edward Weisband, *The Macabresque: Human Violation and Hate in Genocide, Mass Atrocity, and Enemy-Making* (New York: Oxford University Press, 2018).

[14] See, for example, Aleksandar Tišma's novel, *Kapo*, trans. Richard Williams (New York: Harcourt Brace & Company, 1993), which is painful to read.

5 CONCLUSION 97

It seems that the sensationalism that dominates the popular discussion of sexuality and Nazism is mirrored in the pop-psychological explanations of Holocaust survival that continue to pervade the public sphere: Irma Grese on the one hand, Viktor Frankl on the other. The former is a mixture of prurient fascination and enthralled condemnation for a woman combining allure and transgressive violence; the other, a wish-fulfilment fantasy about how positive thinking can get one through adversity, and an avoidance of the grim reality of what people did to survive and the absolute centrality of contingency. In both cases, psychoanalytical terminology and ideas can be dangerously simplistic, channeling analytical rigor into evidence-free zones of pseudo-explanation. On the other hand, in both cases it seems hard not to use psychoanalytical terminology and ideas, not least because the phenomena under description exceed the bounds of the consciously rational. Nazism and the Holocaust may have taken place in the setting of the modern world but they cannot be understood without reference to drives that break with "civilized" behavior. When it comes to explaining survival, psychoanalysis provides easily accessible concepts that can disguise the true nature of what it purportedly explains: identification with the aggressor, Hitler as superego, and so on. On the other hand, psychoanalysis also provides the tools for a sensitive appreciation of survival that speaks to the suppression of "normal" psychological functioning in the context of extreme persecution.

Paula, one of Henry Greenspan's interviewees, recounts at one point how after waking from an Auschwitz nightmare a year after liberation, she wrote in her journal:

> We are the prisoners doomed to death. And I can only call us stupid, ignorant, crazy. Because to live like this—denied everyone and everything, kicked and shoved underfoot, degraded and humiliated, doped and numb—only people who would just as soon be dead could live through this. Having lived it, we are no longer among the living. The living could not survive it.[15]

This statement of being dead in life is confirmation of what Langer calls the "afterdeath of the Holocaust." As Leon Wells wrote: "Dead is dead. It is all gone, completely eradicated, as it was on the first Yom Kippur after

---

[15] Greenspan, *On Listening to Holocaust Survivors*, 83. Paula is a pseudonym for Greenspan's long-term interlocutor, Agi Rubin, about whom he has written elsewhere.

my liberation."[16] But it is also quite impenetrable for a historian, even an oral historian who seeks to understand the past through interviewing people in the present about the past. Here we see that just as psychoanalysis without history cannot provide meaningful insights into social structures and dynamics, so history without psychoanalysis cannot access aspects of the human experience that elude rational thought—and these are sadly many.

---

[16] Leon Wieliczker Wells, *Shattered Faith: A Holocaust Legacy* (Lexington: University Press of Kentucky, 1995), 147.

Bibliography[1]

Abel, Theodore, "The Sociology of Concentration Camps," *Social Forces*, 30:2 (1951), 150–155

Adamczyk, Amy Louise, "Frankl, Bettelheim and the Camps," *Journal of Genocide Research*, 7:1 (2005), 67–84

Adelsberger, Lucie, *Auschwitz: A Doctor's Story* (London: Robson Books, 1996)

Adler, H. G., "Toward a Sociology of the Concentration Camp," *American Journal of Sociology*, 63:5 (1958), 513–522

Adorno, Theodor W., "Freudian Theory and the Pattern of Fascist Propaganda," in *The Culture Industry: Selected Essays on Mass Culture*, ed. J. M. Bernstein (London: Routledge, 2001), 132–157

Alfandary, Rony, *Postmemory, Psychoanalysis and Holocaust Ghosts: The Salonica Cohen Family and Trauma across Generations* (London: Routledge, 2022)

Amir, Marianne, and Rachel Lev-Wiesel, "Time Does Not Heal All Wounds: Quality of Life and Psychological Distress of People Who Survived the Holocaust as Children 55 Years Later," *Journal of Traumatic Stress*, 16:3 (2003), 295–299

---

[1] NB: I have included details here of works that I have read but not cited in the text, in the hope that this bibliography will be a useful resource for those interested in the intersection of psychoanalytic theory and Holocaust historiography.

Ashplant, T. G., "Fantasy, Narrative, Event: Psychoanalysis and History," *History Workshop*, 23 (1987), 165–173
——— "Psychoanalysis in Historical Writing," *History Workshop*, 26 (1988), 102–119
Auerhahn, Nanette C., and Dori Laub, "The Primal Scene of Atrocity: The Dynamic Interplay between Knowledge and Fantasy of the Holocaust in Children of Survivors," *Psychoanalytic Psychology*, 15:3 (1998), 360–377
Ball, Karyn, "Unspeakable Differences, Obscene Pleasures: The Holocaust as an Object of Desire," *Women in German Yearbook*, 19 (2003), 20–49
——— *Disciplining the Holocaust* (Albany: State University of New York Press, 2008)
Barel, Efrat, Abraham Sagi-Schwartz, Marinus H. Van IJzendoorn, and Marian J. Bakermans-Kranenburg, "Surviving the Holocaust: A Meta-Analysis of the Long-Term Sequelae of a Genocide," *Psychological Bulletin*, 136:5 (2010), 677–698
Békés, Vera, J. Christopher Perry, and Claire J. Starrs, "Resilience in Holocaust Survivors: A Study of Defense Mechanisms in Holocaust Narratives," *Journal of Aggression, Maltreatment and Trauma*, 26:10 (2017), 1072–1089
Bellamy, Elizabeth J., *Affective Genealogies: Psychoanalysis, Postmodernism, and the "Jewish Question" after Auschwitz* (Lincoln: University of Nebraska Press, 1997)
Benjamin, Jessica, and Anson Rabinbach, "Foreword," in Klaus Theweleit, *Male Fantasies*, Vol. 2: *Male Bodies, Psychoanalyzing the White Terror* (Minneapolis: University of Minnesota Press, 1989), ix–xxv
Benner, Patricia, Ethel Roskies, and Richard S. Lazarus, "Stress and Coping under Extreme Conditions," in Joel E. Dimsdale, M.D. (ed.), *Survivors, Victims, and Perpetrators: Essays on the Nazi Holocaust* (Washington: Hemisphere Publishing Corporation, 1980), 219–258
Beradt, Charlotte, *The Third Reich of Dreams: The Nightmares of a Nation 1933–1939*, trans. Adriane Gottwald (Wellingborough: The Antiquarian Press, 1985 [1966])
Bergmann, Martin S., "The Jewish and German Roots of Psychoanalysis and the Impact of the Holocaust," *American Imago*, 52:3 (1995), 243–259
Bergmann, Martin S., and Milton E. Jucovy (eds.), *Generations of the Holocaust* (New York: Columbia University Press, 1990)
Bettelheim, Bruno, "Individual and Mass Behaviour in Extreme Situations," *Journal of Abnormal and Social Psychology*, 38 (1943), 417–452
——— *The Informed Heart: A Study of the Psychological Consequences of Living under Extreme Fear and Terror* (Harmondsworth: Penguin Books, 1986a)
——— *Surviving the Holocaust* (London: Fontana, 1986b)
Billinger, Karl, *Fatherland* (New York: International Publishers, 1935)
Bloch, Herbert A., "The Personality of Inmates of Concentration Camps," *American Journal of Sociology*, 52:4 (1947), 335–341

Bluhm, Hilde O., "How Did They Survive? Mechanisms of Defense in Nazi Concentration Camps," *American Journal of Psychotherapy*, 53:1 (1999), 96–122 [orig. *American Journal of Psychotherapy*, 2:1 (1948), 3–32]

Blum, Harold P., "The Intergenerational Taboo of Nazism: A Response and Elaboration of Volker Friedrich's Paper, 'Internalization of Nazism and its Effects on German Psychoanalysts and Their Patients'," *American Imago*, 52:3 (1995), 281–289

Bohleber, Werner, "Remembrance, Trauma, and Collective Memory: The Battle for Memory in Psychoanalysis," *International Journal of Psychoanalysis*, 88:2 (2007), 329–352

―――― *Destructiveness, Intersubjectivity, and Trauma: The Identity Crisis of Modern Psychoanalysis* (London: Routledge, 2010)

―――― "Problems in German Remembrance," in Ira Brenner (ed.), *The Handbook of Psychoanalytic Holocaust Studies: International Perspectives* (London: Routledge, 2020), 129–142

Bolkosky, Sidney M., *Searching for Meaning in the Holocaust* (Westport, CT: Greenwood Press, 2002)

Bollas, Christopher, "The Fascist State of Mind," in *Being a Character: Psychoanalysis and Self Experience* (London: Routledge, 1993), 193–217

Bondy, Curt, "Problems of Internment Camps," *Journal of Abnormal and Social Psychology*, 38:4 (1943), 453–475

Bramstedt, E. K., *Dictatorship and Political Police* (Abingdon: Routledge, 2007 [1945])

Brooks, Peter, and Alex Woloch (eds.), *Whose Freud? The Place of Psychoanalysis in Contemporary Culture* (New Haven: Yale University Press, 2000)

Burney, Christopher, *The Dungeon Democracy* (London: William Heinemann, 1945)

―――― *Solitary Confinement* (London: Clerke and Cockeran, 1952)

Bursztein, Jean-Gérard, *Nazisme et Shoah: Une approche psychanalytique* (Paris: Hermann, 2010)

Chodoff, Paul, "The Holocaust and its Effects on Survivors: An Overview," *Political Psychology*, 18:1 (1997), 147–157

Clifford, Rebecca, *Survivors: Children's Lives after the Holocaust* (New Haven: Yale University Press, 2020)

Cohen, Elie A., *The Abyss: A Confession*, trans. James Brockway (New York: W. W. Norton & Company, 1973)

―――― "The Post-Concentration Camp Syndrome: A Disaster Syndrome," *Science and Public Policy*, 8:3 (1981), 239–246

―――― *Human Behaviour in the Concentration Camp*, trans. M. H. Braaksma (London: Free Association Books, 1988 [1952])

Cohn, Norman, *Warrant for Genocide: The Myth of the Jewish World-Conspiracy and the Protocols of the Elders of Zion* (Harmondsworth: Penguin, 1970)

―――― *Europe's Inner Demons* (Frogmore: Paladin, 1976)

Davidovitch, Nadav, and Rakefet Zalashik, "Recalling the Survivors: Between Memory and Forgetfulness of Hospitalized Holocaust Survivors in Israel," *Israel Studies*, 12:2 (2007), 145–163

Dean, Carolyn J., "Minimalism and Victim Testimony," *History and Theory*, theme issue 49 (2010), 85–99

De Leeuw, Daan, "'In the Name of Humanity': Nazi Doctors and Human Experiments in German Concentration Camps," *Holocaust and Genocide Studies*, 34:2 (2020), 225–252

Deleuze, Gilles, and Félix Guattari, *Anti-Oedipus: Capitalism and Schizophrenia*, trans. Robert Hurley, Mark Seem, and Helen R. Lane (London: Continuum, 2004)

De Wind, E., "The Confrontation with Death," *International Journal of Psycho-analysis*, 49 (1968), 302–305

——— "Psychotherapy after Traumatization Caused by Persecution," *International Psychiatry Clinics*, 8:1 (1971), 93–114

——— "Persecution, Aggression and Therapy," *International Journal of Psycho-analysis*, 53:2 (1972), 173–177

——— "Some Implications of Former Massive Traumatization upon the Actual Analytic Process," *International Journal of Psycho-analysis*, 65:3 (1984), 273–281

——— *Confrontatie met de dood: psychische gevolgen van verfolging* (Utrecht: ICODO, 1993)

——— "Der Experimentierblock," in H. G. Adler, Hermann Langbein and Ella Lingens-Reiner (eds.), *Auschwitz: Zeugnisse und Berichte*, 6th edn (Bonn: Bundeszentrale für politische Bildung, 2014), 175–178

——— *Last Stop Auschwitz: My Story of Survival from within the Camp*, trans. David Colmer (London: Black Swan, 2020)

Di-Capua, Yoav, "Trauma and Other Historians," *Historical Reflections/Réflexions Historiques*, 41:3 (2015), 1–13

Dicks, Henry V., *Licensed Mass Murder: A Socio-Psychological Study of Some SS Killers* (London: Chatto Heinemann, for Sussex University Press, 1972)

Eitinger, Leo, *Concentration Camp Survivors in Norway and Israel* (London: Allen and Unwin, 1964)

——— "Auschwitz—A Psychological Perspective," in Yisrael Gutman and Michael Berenbaum (eds.), *Anatomy of the Auschwitz Death Camp* (Bloomington: Indiana University Press/Washington, DC: United States Holocaust Memorial Museum, 1994), 469–482

Ellmann, Mary, "The Dering Case: A Surgeon at Auschwitz," *Commentary* (July 1964)

Erős, Ferenc, "From War Neurosis to Holocaust Trauma: An Intellectual and Cultural History," *SIMON. Shoah: Intervention, Methods, Documentation*, 4:1 (2017), 41–58

Federn, Ernst, "Essai sur la psychologie de la terreur," *Synthèses: Revue mensuelle internationale*, 7–8 (1946), 79–95
——— "The Terror as a System: The Concentration Camp. Buchenwald as it Was," *Psychiatric Quarterly Supplement*, 22 (1948), 52–86
——— "Versuch einer Psychologie des Terrors," in Roland Kaufhold (ed.), *Ernst Federn—Versuche zur Psychologie des Terrors. Material zum Leben und Werk von Ernst Federn* (Gießen: Psychosozial Verlag, 1998), 35–75
——— *Witnessing Psychoanalysis: From Vienna back to Vienna via Buchenwald and the USA* (Abingdon: Routledge, 2018 [1990])
Fenichel, Otto, "Psychoanalysis of Antisemitism," *American Imago*, 1:2 (1940), 24–39
ffytche, Matt, "Psychoanalytic Sociology and the Traumas of History: Alexander Mitscherlich between the Disciplines," *History of the Human Sciences*, 30:5 (2017), 3–29
Figlio, Karl, *Remembering as Reparation: Psychoanalysis and Historical Memory* (London: Palgrave Macmillan, 2017)
Finchelstein, Federico, *Fascist Mythologies: The History and Politics of Unreason in Borges, Freud, and Schmitt* (New York: Columbia University Press, 2022)
Fisher, David James, "Towards a Psychoanalytic Understanding of Fascism and Anti-Semitism: Perceptions from the 1940s," *Psychoanalysis and History*, 6:1 (2004), 57–74
Fleck, Christian, and Albert Müller, "Bruno Bettelheim and the Concentration Camps," *Journal of the History of the Behavioral Sciences*, 33:1 (1997), 1–37
Foreman, Paul B., "Buchenwald and Modern Prisoner-of-War Detention Policy," *Social Forces*, 37:4 (1959), 289–298
Frankl, Viktor, *Ein Psycholog erlebt das Konzentrationslager* (Vienna: Jugend und Volk, 1946)
——— *From Death-Camp to Existentialism: A Psychiatrist's Path to a New Therapy* (Boston: Beacon Press, 1961)
——— *Man's Search for Meaning* (London: Rider, 2004)
Freud, Anna, "Identification with the Aggressor," in *Selected Writings*, eds. Richard Ekins and Ruth Freeman (London: Penguin, 1998), 13–23
Frey, John R., "Ernst Wiecherts Werk seit 1945," *The German Quarterly*, 22:1 (1949), 37–46
Frie, Roger, *Not in My Family: German Memory and Responsibility after the Holocaust* (New York: Oxford University Press, 2017)
Friedländer, Saul, *L'antisemitisme nazi: histoire d'une psychose collective* (Paris: Éditions du Seuil, 1971)
——— *History and Psychoanalysis* (New York: Holmes & Meier, 1978)
——— *Reflections of Nazism: An Essay on Kitsch and Death* (New York: Avon Books, 1986)

Friedler, Eric, Barbara Siebert, and Andreas Kilian, *Zeugen aus der Todeszone: Das jüdische Sonderkommando in Auschwitz* (Munich: Deutscher Taschenbuch Verlag, 2005)

Friedrich, Volker, "The Internalization of Nazism and its Effects on German Psychoanalysts and Their Patients," *American Imago*, 52:3 (1995), 261–279

Frosh, Stephen, "Psychoanalysis, Nazism and 'Jewish Science'," *The International Journal of Psychoanalysis*, 84:5 (2003), 1315–1332

────── *Hate and the "Jewish Science": Anti-Semitism, Nazism and Psychoanalysis* (Houndmills: Palgrave Macmillan, 2005)

────── "Studies in Prejudice: Theorizing Anti-Semitism in the Wake of the Nazi Holocaust," in Matt ffytche and Daniel Pick (eds.), *Psychoanalysis in the Age of Totalitarianism* (London: Routledge, 2016), 29–41

────── *Antisemitism and Racism: Ethical Challenges for Psychoanalysis* (London: Bloomsbury, 2023)

Garwood, Alfred, *Holocaust Trauma and Psychic Deformation: Psychoanalytic Reflections of a Holocaust Survivor* (London: Routledge, 2017)

Gerson, Samuel, "When the Third is Dead: Memory, Mourning and Witnessing in the Aftermath of the Holocaust," *International Journal of Psychoanalysis*, 90:6 (2009), 1341–1357

Gilman, Sander L., *Freud, Race, and Gender* (Princeton: Princeton University Press, 1993)

Glas-Larson, Margareta, *I Want to Live: The Tragedy and Banality of Survival in Terezin and Auschwitz* (Riverside, CA: Ariadne, 1991)

Goldberg, Amos, *Trauma in First Person: Diary Writing during the Holocaust* (Bloomington: Indiana University Press, 2017)

Greenspan, Henry, *On Listening to Holocaust Survivors: Recounting and Life History* (Westport, CT: Praeger, 1998)

────── "On Testimony, Legacy, and the Problem of Helplessness in History," *Holocaust Studies*, 13:1 (2007), 44–56

────── "Collaborative Interpretation of Survivors' Accounts: A Radical Challenge to Conventional Practice," *Holocaust Studies*, 17:1 (2011), 85–100

────── "The Unsaid, the Incommunicable, the Unbearable, and the Irretrievable," *Oral History Review*, 41:2 (2014a), 229–243

Greenspan, Henry, et al, "Scholars' Forum: Engaging Survivors: Assessing 'Testimony' and 'Trauma' as Foundational Concepts," *Dapim: Studies on the Holocaust*, 28:3 (2014b), 190–226

Grodin, Michael A. (ed.), *Jewish Medical Resistance in the Holocaust* (New York: Berghahn Books, 2014)

Grubrich-Simitis, Ilse, "Extreme Traumatization as Cumulative Trauma," *The Psychoanalytic Study of the Child*, 36 (1981), 415–450

―――― "From Concretism to Metaphor: Thoughts on Some Theoretical and Technical Aspects of the Psychoanalytic Work with Children of Holocaust Survivors," *The Psychoanalytic Study of the Child*, 39 (1984), 301–319

Halpin, Ross W., *Jewish Doctors and the Holocaust: The Anatomy of Survival in Auschwitz* (Berlin: De Gruyter, 2018)

Hartman, John J., "Anna Freud and the Holocaust: Mourning and Survival Guilt," *International Journal of Psychoanalysis*, 95:6 (2014), 1183–1210

Hattwig, Jörg, *Das Dritte Reich im Werk Ernst Wiecherts: Geschichtsdenken, Selbstverständnis und literarische Praxis* (Frankfurt am Main: Peter Lang, 1984)

Hautval, Adélaïde, *Médicine et crimes contre l'humanité: témoignage* (Arles: Actes Sud, 1991)

―――― *Rester humain! Leçons d'Auschwitz et de Ravensbrück* (Paris: Editions Ampelos, 2018)

Heilig, Bruno, *Men Crucified* (London: The Right Book Club, 1942)

Herzog, Dagmar, *Sex after Fascism: Memory and Morality in Twentieth-Century Germany* (Princeton: Princeton University Press, 2005)

―――― "The Obscenity of Objectivity: Post-Holocaust Anti-Semitism and the Invention-Discovery of Post-Traumatic Stress Disorder," in Wendy Lower and Lauren Faulkner Rossi (eds.), *Lessons and Legacies, Vol. XII: New Directions in Holocaust Research and Education* (Evanston: Northwestern University Press, 2017a), 31–63

―――― *Cold War Freud: Psychoanalysis in an Age of Catastrophes* (Cambridge: Cambridge University Press, 2017b)

Herzog, Dagmar (ed.), *Sexuality and German Fascism* (New York: Berghahn Books, 2005)

Heschel, Susannah, "Erotohistoriography: Sensory and Emotional Dimensions of Antisemitism," in Scott Ury and Guy Miron (eds.), *Antisemitism and the Politics of History* (Waltham, MA: Brandeis University Press, 2023), 65–86

Hill, Mavis M., and L. Norman Williams, *Auschwitz in England: A Record of a Libel Action* (London: MacGibbon & Kee, 1965)

Horkheimer, Max, and Samuel H. Flowerman, "Foreword to Studies in Prejudice," in T. W. Adorno, Else Frenkel-Brunswik, Daniel J. Levinson and R. Nevitt Sanford, *The Authoritarian Personality*, abridged edn (New York: W.W. Norton & Company, 1982 [1950]), vii–x

Jacobson, Edith, "Observations on the Psychological Effect of Imprisonment on Female Political Prisoners," in K. R. Eissler (ed.), *Searchlights on Delinquency: New Psychoanalytic Studies* (London: Imago Publishing Co., 1949), 341–368

Jackman, Norman R., "Survival in the Concentration Camp," *Human Organization*, 17:2 (1958), 23–26

Jaffe, Ruth, "The Sense of Guilt within Holocaust Survivors," *Jewish Social Studies*, 32:4 (1970), 307–314

Kahn, Laurence, *What Nazism Did to Psychoanalysis* (London: Routledge, 2023)

Kalmar, Rudolf, *Zeit ohne Gnade* (Vienna: J&V Edition Wien, 1988 [1946])
Kansteiner, Wulf, "Testing the Limits of Trauma: The Long-Term Psychological Effects of the Holocaust on Individuals and Collectives," *History of the Human Sciences*, 17:2–3 (2004), 97–123
Kanter, Isaac, "Extermination Camp Syndrome: The Delayed Type of Double-Bind," *International Journal of Social Psychiatry*, 16:4 (1970), 275–282
Karst, George M., *The Beasts of the Earth*, trans. Emil Lengyel (New York: Albert Unger, 1942)
Karydaki, Danae, *Mapping "Man's Inhumanity to Man": A Historical and Historiographical Investigation into the Columbus Centre for the Study of Persecution and Genocide (University of Sussex, 1962–1981)*, PhD thesis (Birkbeck, University of London, 2016a)
——— "National Socialism and the English Genius: Revisiting George Orwell's Political Views on Nazi Ideology," *Dapim: Studies on the Holocaust*, 30:1 (2016b), 53–73
——— "Nazism's Inner Demons: Psychoanalysis and the Columbus Centre (1962–1981)," in Shmuel Bar-Haim, Elizabeth Sarah Coles, and Helen Tyson (eds.), *Wild Analysis: From the Couch to Cultural and Political Life* (London: Routledge, 2022), 147–164
——— *History and Psychoanalysis in the Columbus Centre: the Meaning of Evil* (London: Routledge, 2023)
Kautsky, Benedikt, *Devils and the Damned*, trans. Kenneth Case (London: Brown, Watson, Ltd., 1960)
Kay, Avi, "The Impact of Attitudes toward the Holocaust and Holocaust Survivors in the United States, on the Adult Psychological Development of American Holocaust Survivors," in Johannes-Dieter Steinert and Inge Weber-Newth (eds.), *Beyond Camps and Forced Labour: Current International Research on Survivors of Nazi Persecution* (Osnabrück: Secolo, 2005), 596–607
Kay, G. R., *Dachau: The Nazi Hell. From the Notes of a Former Prisoner at the Notorious Nazi Concentration Camp* (London: Francis Aldor, 1939)
Kearns, Katherine, *Psychoanalysis, Historiography and Feminist Theory: The Search for Critical Method* (Cambridge: Cambridge University Press, 1997)
Keilson, Hans, "Sequential Traumatization of Children," *Danish Medical Bulletin*, 27:5 (1980), 235–237
——— *Wohin die Sprache nicht reicht: Vorträge und Essays aus dem Jahren 1936–1996* (Gießen: J. Richer'sche Universitäts-Buchhandlung, 1998)
Kestenberg, Judith S., "Psychoanalyses of Children of Survivors from the Holocaust: Case Presentations and Assessment," *Journal of the American Psychoanalytic Association*, 28:4 (1980), 775–804
Kirshner, Lewis A., "Trauma, the Good Object, and the Symbolic: A Theoretical Integration," *International Journal of Psycho-Analysis*, 75:2 (1994), 235–242

―――― "Trauma and Psychosis: A Review and Framework for Psychoanalytic Understanding," *International Forum for Psychoanalysis* (2013), 1–9
Klapper, John, "Cultural 'Diskontinuität' and Thematic Continuity: Ernst Wiechert after 1945," *German Life and Letters*, 62:4 (2009), 430–447
―――― "Disputed Nonconformist and 'Zwischenreichautor': A Reassessment of Ernst Wiechert's Life and Work in Nazi Germany," *Oxford German Studies*, 39:3 (2010), 250–270
―――― "Dissent and Cultural Pessimism in Ernst Wiechert's 'Die weiße Büffel oder Von der großen Gerechtigkeit': 'Inner Emigration' under National Socialism," *The German Quarterly*, 90:1 (2017), 19–35
Klein, Melanie, *The Psycho-Analysis of Children* (London: Virago Press, 1989)
Kohut, Thomas A., *A German Generation: An Experiential History of the Twentieth Century* (New Haven: Yale University Press, 2012)
Kopstein, Jeffrey S., Jelena Subotić, and Susan Welch (eds.), *Politics, Violence, Memory: The New Social Science of the Holocaust* (Ithaca: Cornell University Press, 2023)
Krell, Robert, "Resilience," in Ira Brenner (ed.), *The Handbook of Psychoanalytic Holocaust Studies: International Perspectives* (London: Routledge, 2020), 41–51
Krell, Robert, and Marc I. Sherman (eds.), *Medical and Psychological Effects of Concentration Camps on Holocaust Survivors* (New Brunswick: Transaction Publishers, 1997)
Kuntz, Benjamin, *Lucie Adelsberger: Doctor—Scientist—Chronicler of Auschwitz* (Berlin: Hentrich und Hentrich, 2021)
Krystal, Henry (ed.), *Massive Psychic Trauma* (New York: International Universities Press, 1968)
Kuby, Emma, *Political Survivors: The Resistance, the Cold War, and the Fight against Concentration Camps after 1945* (Ithaca: Cornell University Press, 2019)
Kuriloff, Emily A., "The Holocaust and Psychoanalytic Theory and Practice," *Contemporary Psychoanalysis*, 46:3 (2010), 395–422
―――― *Contemporary Psychoanalysis and the Legacy of the Third Reich: History, Memory, Tradition* (New York: Routledge, 2014)
Kuschey, Bernhard, *Die Ausnahme des Überlebens. Ernst und Hilde Federn: Eine biographische Studie und eine Analyse der Binnenstrukturen des Konzentrationslagers*, 2 vols. (Gießen: Psychosozial Verlag, 2003)
―――― "Der Terrorpsychologe, Historiker der Psychoanalyse und Pionier der psychoanalytischen Sozialarbeit Ernst Federn. Eine Werkbiographie," *Zeitschrift für psychoanalytische Theorie und Praxis*, 19:4 (2004), 390–398
LaCapra, Dominick, *History and Memory after Auschwitz* (Ithaca: Cornell University Press, 1998)
―――― *Writing History, Writing Trauma* (Baltimore: Johns Hopkins University Press, 2001)

Lang, Hans-Joachim, *Die Frauen von Block 10: Medizinische Versuche in Auschwitz* (Augsburg: Weltbild, 2018)
Langbein, Hermann, *Die Stärkeren: Ein Bericht aus Auschwitz und anderen Konzentrationslagern* (Vienna: Ephelant Verlag, 2008)
Langer, Lawrence L., *Versions of Survival: The Holocaust and the Human Spirit* (Albany, NY: State University of New York Press, 1982)
Langhoff, Wolfgang, *Rubber Truncheon: Being an Account of Thirteen Months Spent in a Concentration Camp*, trans. Lilo Linke (London: Constable & Co., 1935)
Laub, Dori, "Traumatic Shutdown of Narrative and Symbolization: A Death Instinct Derivative?," *Contemporary Psychoanalysis*, 41:2 (2005a), 307–326
—— "From Speechlessness to Narrative: The Case of Holocaust Historians and of Psychiatrically Hospitalized Survivors," *Literature and Medicine*, 24:2 (2005b), 253–265
Laub, Dori, and Nanette C. Auerhahn, "Failed Empathy—A Central Theme in the Survivor's Holocaust Experience," *Psychoanalytic Psychology*, 6:4 (1989), 377–400
—— "Holocaust Testimony," *Holocaust and Genocide Studies*, 5:4 (1990), 447–462
Laub, Dori, and Andreas Hamburger (eds.), *Psychoanalysis and Holocaust Testimony: Unwanted Memories of Social Trauma* (London: Routledge, 2017)
Laub, Dori, and Susanna Lee, "Thanatos and Massive Social Trauma: The Impact of the Death Instinct on Knowing, Remembering, and Forgetting," *Journal of the American Psychoanalytic Association*, 51:2 (2003), 433–464
Leschnitzer, Adolf, *The Magic Background of Modern Anti-Semitism: An Analysis of the German-Jewish Relationship* (New York: International Universities Press, 1969 [1956])
Lifton, Robert Jay, "The Image of 'The End of the World': A Psychohistorical View," in Saul Friedländer, Gerald Holton, Leo Marx, and Eugene Skolnikoff (eds.), *Visions of Apocalypse: End or Rebirth* (New York: Holmes & Meier, 1985), 151–167
Lindeman, Yehudi, "Abandonment, Adjustment, and Memory: Reflections on J. Presser, Elie Cohen and Gerhard Durlacher," in Wolfgang Mieder and David Scrase (eds.), *Reflections on the Holocaust: Festschrift for Raul Hilberg on his Seventy-Fifth Birthday* (Burlington, VT: The Center for Holocaust Studies at the University of Vermont, 2001), 79–97
Lingens-Reiner, Ella, *Prisoners of Fear* (London: Victor Gollancz, 1948)
Lobonț, Florin, *Mind, Philosophy, History, and Psychoanalysis: Essays on Historical Understanding* (Bucharest: Trei, 2014)
—— "Conceptual Idealism and Emotional Reasoning," *International Journal of Philosophical Practice*, 9:1 (2023), 158–172

Loewenau, Aleksandra, *The Impact of Nazi Medical Experiments on Polish Inmates at Dachau, Auschwitz and Ravensbrück*, PhD thesis, Oxford Brookes University (2012)
Loewenberg, Peter, "The Psychohistorical Origins of the Nazi Youth Cohort," *American Historical Review*, 76:5 (1971a), 1457–1502
—— "The Unsuccessful Adolescence of Heinrich Himmler," *American Historical Review*, 76:3 (1971b), 612–641
—— "Psychohistorical Perspectives on Modern German History," *Journal of Modern History*, 47:2 (1975), 229–279
—— *Fantasy and Reality in History* (New York: Oxford University Press, 1995)
Loewenstein, Era A., "In Dark Times: Psychoanalytic Praxis as a Form of Resistance to Fascist Propaganda," *Psychoanalytic Inquiry*, 43:2 (2023), 130–144
Loewenstein, Rudolph M., *Christians and Jews: A Psychoanalytic Study* (New York: International Universities Press, 1952)
Lomranz, Jacob, "The Skewed Image of the Holocaust Survivor and the Vicissitudes of Holocaust Research," *Echoes of the Holocaust: Bulletin of the Jerusalem Center for Research into the Late Effects of the Holocaust*, 6 (2000), 45–57
Lorska, Dorota, "Block 10 in Auschwitz," in Hamburger Institut für Sozialforschung (ed.), *Die Auschwitz-Hefte. Vol. 1: Texte der polnischen Zeitschrift "Przegląd Lekarski" über historische, psychische und medizinische Aspekte des Lebens und Sterbens in Auschwitz* (Rogner & Bernhard Verlag), 209–212
Luchterhand, Elmer, "Prisoner Behavior and Social System in the Nazi Concentration Camps," *International Journal of Social Psychology*, 13 (1964), 245–264
Luel, Steve A., and Paul Marcus (eds.), *Psychoanalytic Reflections on the Holocaust: Selected Essays* (New York: Ktav Publishing House, 1984)
Maidenbaum, Aryeh, and Stephen A. Martin (eds.), *Lingering Shadows: Jungians, Freudians, and Anti-Semitism* (Boston: Shambhala, 1991)
Mandel, Naomi, "Speaking Corpses and Spectral Spaces: Representing Testimony after the Holocaust," *Dialectical Anthropology*, 24:3–4 (1999), 357–376
Maniadakis, Grigoris, "On Survival," *International Forum of Psychoanalysis*, 31:3 (2022), 129–131
Marcus, Paul, *Autonomy in the Extreme Situation: Bruno Bettelheim, the Nazi Concentration Camps, and the Mass Society* (Westport, CT: Praeger, 1999)
Marcus, Paul, and Alan Rosenberg, "Reevaluating Bruno Bettelheim's Work on the Nazi Concentration Camps," *The Psychoanalytic Review*, 81:3 (1994), 537–563
McGowan, Todd, *The Racist Fantasy: Unconscious Roots of Hatred* (London: Bloomsbury, 2022)
Micheels, Louis J., "Bearer of the Secret," *Psychoanalytic Inquiry*, 5:1 (1985), 21–30

———— *Doctor #117641: A Holocaust Memoir* (New Haven: Yale University Press, 1989)

Minney, R. J., *I Shall Fear No Evil: The Story of Alina Brewda's Survival in Auschwitz* (London: Corgi, 1967)

Mitchell, Stephen A., and Margaret J. Black (eds.), *Freud and Beyond: A History of Modern Psychoanalytic Thought* (New York: Basic Books, 1995)

Moss, Donald, "On Hating in the First Person Plural: Thinking Psychoanalytically about Racism, Homophobia, and Misogyny," *Journal of the American Psychoanalytic Association*, 49:4 (2001), 1315–1354

Neurath, Paul Martin, *The Society of Terror: Inside the Buchenwald and Dachau Concentration Camps* (London: Routledge, 2005)

Niederland, William G., "The Problem of the Survivor," *Journal of the Hillside Hospital*, 10:3–4 (1961), 233–247

———— "Clinical Observations on the 'Survivor Syndrome'," *International Journal of Psychoanalysis*, 49 (1968), 313–315

———— "The Survivor Syndrome: Further Observations and Dimensions," *Journal of the American Psychoanalytic Association*, 29:2 (1981), 413–425

Niven, Bill, "Ernst Wiechert and His Role between 1933 and 1945," *New German Studies*, 16 (1990), 1–20

Nutkiewicz, Michael, "Shame, Guilt, and Anguish in Holocaust Survivor Testimony," *Oral History Review*, 30:1 (2003), 1–22

Ornstein, Anna, "Survival and Recovery," *Psychoanalytic Inquiry*, 5:1 (1985), 99–130

———— "Mass Murder and the Individual: Psychoanalytic Reflections on Perpetrators and Their Victims," *International Journal of Group Psychotherapy*, 62:1 (2012), 1–20

Perl, Gisella, *I Was a Doctor in Auschwitz* (New York: International Universities Press, 1948)

Pick, Daniel, *The Pursuit of the Nazi Mind: Hitler, Hess, and the Analysts* (Oxford: Oxford University Press, 2012)

———— *Psychoanalysis: A Very Short Introduction* (Oxford: Oxford University Press, 2015)

Pinchevski, Amit, "The Audiovisual Unconscious: Media and Trauma in the Video Archive for Holocaust Testimonies," *Critical Inquiry*, 39:1 (2012), 142–166

Pinchevski, Amit, and Tamar Liebes, "Severed Voices: Radio and the Mediation of Trauma in the Eichmann Trial," *Public Culture*, 22:2 (2010), 265–291

Poliakov, Léon, *The Aryan Myth: A History of Racist and Nationalist Ideas in Europe* (London: Chatto Heinemann for Sussex University Press, 1974)

Prince, Robert, "Psychoanalysis Traumatized: The Legacy of the Holocaust," *The American Journal of Psychoanalysis*, 69:3 (2009a), 179–194

———— "The Self in Pain: The Paradox of Memory. The Paradox of Testimony," *The American Journal of Psychoanalysis*, 69:4 (2009b), 279–290

Pytell, Timothy, "The Missing Pieces of the Puzzle: A Reflection on the Odd Career of Viktor Frankl," *Journal of Contemporary History*, 35:2 (2000), 281–306

────── "Redeeming the Unredeemable: Auschwitz and *Man's Search for Meaning*," *Holocaust and Genocide Studies*, 17:1 (2003), 89–113

────── "Extreme Experience, Psychological Insight, and Holocaust Perception: Reflections on Bettelheim and Frankl," *Psychoanalytic Psychology*, 24:4 (2007), 641–657

────── "Viktor Frankl's Flight into the Spiritual," in Zeev Mankowitz, David Weinberg, and Sharon Kangisser Cohen (eds.), *Europe in the Eyes of Survivors of the Holocaust* (Jerusalem: Yad Vashem, 2014), 127–146

────── *Viktor Frankl's Search for Meaning: An Emblematic 20th-Century Life* (New York: Berghahn Books, 2015)

Redles, David, "The Apocalypse of Adolf Hitler: *Mein Kampf* and the Eschatological Origins of the Holocaust," in John J. Michalczyk, Michael S. Bryant, and Susan A. Michalczyk (eds.), *Hitler's Mein Kampf and the Holocaust: A Prelude to Genocide* (London: Bloomsbury, 2022), 213–233

Reijzer, Hans, *A Dangerous Legacy: Judaism and the Psychoanalytic Movement* (London: Routledge, 2018)

Reiner, Guido, *Ernst Wiechert im Dritten Reich: Eine Dokumentation* (Paris: Selbstverlag, 1974)

Rickels, Laurence A., *Nazi Psychoanalysis, Vol. 1: Only Psychoanalysis Won the War* (Minneapolis: University of Minnesota Press, 2002a)

────── *Nazi Psychoanalysis, Vol. 2: Crypto-Fetishism* (Minneapolis: University of Minnesota Press, 2002b)

Roazen, Paul, *The Historiography of Psychoanalysis* (London: Routledge, 2001)

────── "The Rise and Fall of Bruno Bettelheim," *The Psychohistory Review*, 20:3 (1992), 221–250

Robinson, S. et al, "The Late Effects of Nazi Persecution among Elderly Holocaust Survivors," *Acta Psychiatrica Scandinavica*, 82 (1990), 311–315

Romney, Claude, "Jewish Medical Resistance in Block 10, Auschwitz," in Michael A. Grodin (ed.), *Jewish Medical Resistance in the Holocaust* (New York: Berghahn Books, 2014), 185–196

Roper, Michael, "Analysing the Analysed: Transference and Counter-Transference in the Oral History Encounter," *Oral History*, 31:2 (2003), 20–32

────── "Psychoanalysis and the Making of History," in Nancy Partner and Sarah R. I. Foot (eds.), *The Sage Handbook of Historical Theory* (London: Sage, 2013), 311–325

Rosenbaum, Ron, *Explaining Hitler: The Search for the Origins of His Evil* (London: Macmillan, 1998)

Rousset, David, *L'univers concentrationnaire* (Paris: Éditions de Minuit, 1993 [1946])

—— *A World Apart*, trans. Yvonne Moyse and Roger Senhouse (London: Secker and Warburg, 1951 [1946])

Rousseau, Cécile, "Diving into Complexity: John Sigal's Work on the Long-term Consequences of the Holocaust," *Clinical Child Psychology and Psychiatry*, 10:2 (2005), 262–265

Santner, Eric L., *Stranded Objects: Mourning, Memory, and Film in Postwar Germany* (Ithaca: Cornell University Press, 1990)

Schmidt, Christine, "'Privilege' and Trauma: Sieg Maandag's Climb Upwards," *American Imago*, 80:1 (2023), 81–106

Schrage, Franz H., *Weimar—Buchenwald: Spuren nationalsozialistischer Vernichtungsgewalt in Werken von Ernst Wiechert, Eugen Kogon, Jorge Semprun* (Düsseldorf: Grupello Verlag, 1999)

Seidlin, Oskar, "Begegnung mit Ernst Wiechert," *The German Quarterly*, 19:4 (1946), 270–273

Shelley, Lore (ed.), *Criminal Experiments on Human Beings in Auschwitz and War Research Laboratories: Twenty Women Prisoners' Accounts* (San Francisco: Mellen Research University Press, 1991)

Shmotkin, Dov, Amit Shrira, Shira C. Goldberg, and Yuval Palgi, "Resilience and Vulnerability among Aging Holocaust Survivors and Their Families: An Intergenerational Overview," *Journal of Intergenerational Relationships*, 9:1 (2011), 7–21

Siegel, Sari J., "Treating an Auschwitz Prisoner-Physician: The Case of Dr. Maximilian Samuel," *Holocaust and Genocide Studies*, 28:3 (2014), 450–481

—— "The Past and Promise of Jewish Prisoner-Physicians' Accounts," *SIMON: Shoah: Intervention, Methods, Documentation*, 3:1 (2016), 89–103

—— "The Coercion-Resistance Spectrum: Analyzing Prisoner-Functionary Behaviour in Nazi Camps," *Journal of Genocide Research*, 23:1 (2021), 17–36

Sigal, John J., and Vivian Rakoff, "Concentration Camp Survival: A Pilot Study of Effects on the Second Generation," *Canadian Psychiatric Association Journal*, 16:5 (1971), 393–397

Simenauer, Erich, "A Double Helix: Some Determinants of the Self-Perpetuation of Naziism," *The Psychoanalytic Study of the Child*, 33 (1978), 411–425

Spiegel, Rose, "Survival, Psychoanalysis and the Third Reich," *The Journal of the American Academy of Psychoanalysis*, 13:4 (1985), 521–536

Spiegel, Rose, Gerard Chrzanowski and Arthur H. Feiner, "On Psychoanalysis in the Third Reich," *Contemporary Psychoanalysis*, 11:4 (1975), 477–510

Sterba, Editha, "Emotional Problems of Displaced Children," *Journal of Social Casework*, 30 (1949), 175–181

Stern, Judith, "The Eichmann Trial and its Influence on Psychiatry and Psychology," *Theoretical Inquiries in Law*, 1:2 (2000), 393–428

Steinert, Johannes-Dieter, and Dan Stone (eds.), *Britain and Holocaust Consciousness in the 1960s* (London: Bloomsbury, forthcoming 2025)
Stone, Dan, "Sieg Maandag and Holocaust Art," *American Imago*, 80:1 (2023a), 23–42
—— *The Holocaust: An Unfinished History* (London: Penguin, 2023b)
—— *Fate Unknown: Tracing the Missing after World War II and the Holocaust* (Oxford: Oxford University Press, 2023c)
—— "The Two Faces of the 'Final Solution': Popular Holocaust Memory and Holocaust Historiography," in Wulf Kansteiner and Christina Morina (eds.), *The Oxford Handbook of History and Memory* (Oxford: Oxford University Press, forthcoming-a)
—— "In(ani)mate Objects: Between the Sacred and the Everyday," *MAVCOR Journal* (forthcoming-b)
—— "The Historiography of the Holocaust: The Years of Diversification and Integration," in Mark Roseman and Dan Stone (eds.), *The Cambridge History of the Holocaust*, Vol. 1 (Cambridge: Cambridge University Press, forthcoming-c)
—— "Female Inmate-Physicians of Block 10 at Auschwitz as Witnesses at the Dering v. Uris Libel Trial," in Johannes-Dieter Steinert and Dan Stone (eds.), *Britain and Holocaust Consciousness in the 1960s* (London: Bloomsbury, forthcoming-d)
—— "When the Nineteenth Century Ended for Jews: The Elderly and the Holocaust," in Elizabeth Anthony, Joanna Sliwa and Christine Schmidt (eds.), *Older Jews and the Holocaust* (Detroit: Wayne State University Press, forthcoming-e)
Szalet, Leon, *Experiment "E": A Report from an Extermination Laboratory* (New York: Didier, 1945)
Szende, Stefan, *The Promise Hitler Kept*, trans. Edward Fitzgerald (London: Victor Gollancz, 1945)
Szmaglewska, Seweryna, *Smoke over Birkenau*, trans. Jadwiga Rynas (Oświęcim: Auschwitz-Birkenau State Museum, 2001 [1947])
Szwarc, Halina, "The Premature Ageing of Former KZ-Prisoners," *Zeitschrift für Alternsforschung*, 40:4 (1985), 209–212
Tas, J., "Psychical Disorders among Inmates of Concentration Camps and Repatriates," *The Psychiatric Quarterly*, 25:4 (1951), 679–690
Timms, Edward, and Naomi Segal (eds.), *Freud in Exile: Psychoanalysis and its Vicissitudes* (New Haven: Yale University Press, 1988)
Trautman, Edgar C., "Violence and Victims in Nazi Concentration Camps and the Psychopathology of the Survivors," *International Psychiatry Clinics*, 8:1 (1971), 115–131
Trezise, Thomas, *Witnessing Witnessing: On the Reception of Holocaust Survivor Testimony* (New York: Fordham University Press, 2013)

Utitz, Emil, *Psychologie des Lebens im Konzentrationslager Theresienstadt* (Vienna: Verlag A. Sexl, 1948)

van IJzendoorn, Marinus H., Marian J. Bakermans-Kranenburg, and Abraham Sagi-Schwartz, "Are Children of Holocaust Survivors Less Well-Adapted? A Meta-Analytic Investigation of Secondary Traumatization," *Journal of Traumatic Stress*, 16:5 (2003), 459–469

von Fransecky, Tanja, *Escapees: The History of Jews Who Fled Nazi Deportation Trains in France, Belgium and The Netherlands* (New York: Berghahn Books, 2019)

Weindling, Paul, *Victims and Survivors of Nazi Human Experiments: Science and Suffering in the Holocaust* (London: Bloomsbury, 2015)

Weisband, Edward, *The Macabresque: Human Violation and Hate in Genocide, Mass Atrocity, and Enemy-Making* (New York: Oxford University Press, 2018)

Wesełucha, Piotr, "The Concentration Camp as a Psychiatric Experiment," *Przegląd Lekarski—Oświęcim*, 1970; *Medical Review Auschwitz*, 2017: https://www.mp.pl/auschwitz/journal/english/170032,the-concentration-camp-as-a-psychiatric-experiment

Wiechert, Ernst, *The Forest of the Dead*, trans. Ursula Stechow (London: Victor Gollancz, 1947)

——— *Der Totenwald: Ein Bericht* (Leipzig: Reclam, 1989)

Wiedemann, Frank, *Psychologen im Konzentrationslager—Methoden und Strategien des Überlebens* (Frankfurt am Main: Peter Lang, 2017)

Wolffheim, Nelly, "Kinder aus Konzentrationslagern," in *Psychoanalyse und Kindergarten und andere Arbeiten zur Kinderpsychologie*, eds. Gerd Biermann and Horst-Eberhard Richter (Munich: Ernst Reinhardt Verlag, 1973), 192–263

Wünschmann, Kim, "The 'Scientification' of the Concentration Camp: Early Theories of Terror and Their Reception by American Academia," *Leo Baeck Institute Yearbook*, 58 (2013), 111–126

Zajde, Nathalie, "The Psychiatric Treatment of Holocaust Survivors, or, the Tribulations of a Syndrome," in Jean-Marc Dreyfus and Daniel Langton (eds.), *Writing the Holocaust* (London: Bloomsbury Academic, 2011a), 62–75

——— "The Holocaust and the Limits of Psychoanalysis: The Case of Bruno Bettelheim," in Jean-Marc Dreyfus and Daniel Langton (eds.), *Writing the Holocaust* (London: Bloomsbury Academic, 2011b), 116–135

Index[1]

A
Adelsberger, Lucie, 45
Adler, H. G., 25, 45
Adorno, T. W., 4, 16, 40
American Journal of Psychotherapy, 66, 67
Antisemitism, 5, 93, 94
Arendt, Hannah, 33
"Asocials", 75, 80, 87
Auschwitz
  Birkenau, 48, 50, 51, 58, 73
  Frankfurt trial, 87
  Monowitz, 35
  Sonderkommando in, 58, 61

B
Ball, Karyn, 7, 46, 47
Belsen, 37n66, 86
Benner, Patricia, 37

Bergmann, Martin, 92
Bettelheim, Bruno, 11–13, 20–25, 22n7, 22n10, 31, 32, 39, 40, 44, 61, 62, 67, 67n2, 72–75, 81, 83, 87
Billinger, Karl, 67
Black, Margaret J., 72
Bloch, Herbert, 79
Bluhm, Hilde O., 20, 21, 34, 66–89, 93
Boder, David, 10
Bohleber, Werner, 9, 29, 69
Bondy, Curt, 13
Brewda, Alina, 40, 44, 45, 48–52, 54–59, 61
Buchenwald, 11, 13, 22, 73, 74, 77, 83, 86
Burney, Christopher, 67, 80, 81

---

[1] Note: Page numbers followed by 'n' refer to notes.

INDEX

C
Caplan, Jane, 96
Clauberg, Hans, 48–50, 57, 59
Clifford, Rebecca, 7
Cohen, Elie A., 20, 23, 25, 31–37, 39, 40, 44, 46, 50, 60, 62, 92
Commentary, 80
Concentration camp syndrome, 14, 39
Countertransference, 8, 15
Cyprus, 53

D
Dachau, 22, 41, 86
Dean, Carolyn, 7
Dering, Władysław, 45, 48, 51–58
Des Pres, Terrence, 23
De Wind, Eddy, 8n20, 20–42, 44, 46, 48–50, 61, 62, 69, 72, 75, 83, 89, 92
Duncan, Colin, 55, 57, 59
Durlacher, Gerhard, 37

E
Ebsworth, John David, 55
Ego psychology, 71, 72
Eichmann, Adolf, 45, 53, 87
  trial of, 53, 87
Eitinger, Leo, 8n20, 13, 13n36, 62, 69
Estrangement, 13, 69, 72, 73, 75, 83, 88, 89

F
Fascism, 3, 4, 96
Federn, Ernst, 7n19, 11, 22, 22n10, 67, 76, 77, 87
Federn, Paul, 22
Fenichel, Otto, 93
Ferenczi, Sándor, 11, 12

Fleck, Christian, 11–13, 67n2
Flowerman, Samuel H., 40
Fortunoff Archive for video testimony, 9
Frankl, Viktor, 7n19, 20, 21, 24, 25, 31, 32, 34, 39, 40, 44, 67, 72–74, 79, 83, 87, 97
Freeman, Elizabeth, 96
Freud, Anna, 11, 12
Freud, Sigmund, 16, 26, 29, 38, 69–72, 85
Freud, Sophie, 68
Friedländer, Saul, 5
Fromm, Erich, 6, 96
Furst, Sidney, 8, 9

G
Gardiner, Lord, 54–57
Glas-Larsson, Margaret, 21
Goering Institute, 4
Goldberg, Amos, 6
Grabczynski, Dr, 55
Greenspan, Henry, 11, 83, 85, 88, 97, 97n15
Grese, Irma, 97
Gross-Rosen, 84
Grubman, Sally, 11
Grubrich-Simitis, Ilse, 76
Guterman, Norbert, 80

H
Haffner, Sebastian, 6
Hamburger, Andreas, 4, 14
Hartman, Geoffrey, 9
Hartmann, Heinz, 72
Hautval, Adélaïde, 40, 44, 45, 49–59, 61, 62
Heinemann, Elizabeth, 96
Herzog, Dagmar, 7, 96
Heschel, Susannah, 96

Hewer, Christopher, 55
Hilberg, Raul, 94
Hill, Mavis, 48, 52, 54, 57
Hitler, Adolf, 5, 6, 97
Horkheimer, Max, 40

I
Identification with the aggressor, 11–13, 71, 79, 81, 82, 84, 97
Irving, David, 54
Israel, 53, 87, 92, 94

J
Jackman, Norman R., 31n38

K
Kabeli, I., 61
Kahn, Laurence, 9, 29, 70
Kalmar, Rudolf, 67, 76
Kaplan, Chaim, 6, 46n8
Kapos, 13, 79, 82, 87
Karst, George M., 67, 78
Kautsky, Benedikt, 67, 67n2, 79, 81–83, 87, 89
Kay, Avi, 15
Keilson, Hans, 8n20, 20
Klemperer, Victor, 6, 46n8
Klodzinski, Stanislaw, 55
Krebs, Berthold, 33
Krell, Robert, 22, 83
Krystal, Henry, 8, 8n20, 28, 29, 39, 41, 85
Kuriloff, Emily, 24, 30, 31, 92

L
LaCapra, Dominick, 8, 94, 95
Langbein, Hermann, 25, 45, 50, 51, 55

Langer, Lawrence, 21, 40, 58, 59, 97
Laub, Dori, 9, 85
Lawton, Mr Justice, 55
Lazarus, Richard S., 37
Lengyel, Olga, 45
Lenzing, 80
Levi, Primo, 37, 66, 79
Lifton, Robert, 28
Lindeman, Yehudi, 37
Lingens-Reiner, Ella, 25, 40, 45, 58, 61
Lipstadt, Deborah, 54
Littell, Jonathan, 95
Loewenberg, Peter, 5
Loewenstein, Rudolph M., 93
Lomranz, Jacob, 39, 42
Lorska, Dorota, 39, 44, 45, 49–52, 54–59, 61

M
Majdanek, 55, 84
Marcus, Paul, 61
Mechelen, 35
Meerloo, Joost, 76
Memory studies, 7
Micheels, Louis, 20, 25, 33–36, 39, 40, 44, 46, 50, 59, 62, 92
Minney, R. J., 56, 57
Mitchell, Stephen A., 72
Mitscherlich, Alexander, 4
Mitscherlich, Margarete, 4
Mosse, George L., 96
Müller, Albert, 11–13

N
Nazism, 3–6, 24, 87, 95–97
Neustadt-Glewe, 52
Niederland, W. G., 3, 8, 8n20, 14, 24, 28, 39, 41, 69, 76
Niven, Bill, 75

Nixon, William, 55
November pogrom, 86
Nutkiewicz, Michael, 47

O
Oedipus complex, 2, 35
Ornstein, Anna, 8n20, 24, 31

P
Penguin Books, 54
Perl, Gisella, 45
Pick, Daniel, 7
Pinchevski, Amit, 10
Post-traumatic stress disorder (PTSD), 3, 4, 14, 25, 27, 28, 39, 41, 42, 70, 85
  See also Trauma
Pressburger, Emeric, 45
Presser, Jacques, 33
Przegląd Lekarski – Oświęcim, 38, 51
Psychiatric Quarterly, 37n66, 77
Psychohistory, 5
PTSD, *see* Post-traumatic stress disorder

R
Rapaport, Ernest, 2
Ravensbrück, 52
Red Army, 52, 86
Reich, Wilhelm, 6, 96
Reijzer, Hans, 24
Resilience, 14, 29, 88, 92
Roskies, Ethel, 37
Rousset, David, 63, 67, 78–81
Rwanda, 14

S
Sachsenhausen, 66, 73, 86
Sadism, 6, 78

Santner, Eric L., 4, 93, 94
Stern, Judith, 92
Stonehill, John, 10
Survivor syndrome, 4, 14, 24, 28, 29, 42, 92
Synthèses (Brussels), 77
Szalet, Leon, 66, 67, 78, 80
Szende, Stefan, 16
Szmaglewska, Seweryna, 67, 81, 82, 89

T
Tas, Jacques, 27, 37n66
Terry, Jack, 2
Testimony, 9–11, 15, 24, 44, 48, 54, 57–59, 93
  See also Video testimony
Trauma, 2, 4, 6, 8, 8n20, 9, 11, 14, 15, 20, 25, 27, 29, 30, 38, 39, 41, 42, 47, 69–71, 73, 77, 78, 84, 85, 88, 89, 92, 94
  See also Post-traumatic stress disorder (PTSD)
Treblinka, 83

U
Unconscious, 2, 5, 9, 29, 41, 72
Uris, Leon, 52, 53, 55, 56, 58
Utitz, Emil, 38, 40

V
Video testimony, 9–11, 15
Vietnam War, 27

W
Wells, Leon, 97
Westerbork, 20, 25, 32
West Germany, 2, 15, 30
  restitution claims, 2

Wiechert, Ernst, 67, 68, 73–77, 75n29, 79, 80
Williams, Norman L., 48, 52, 54, 57
Windeyer, Brian, 55
Wirths, Christian, 45, 50, 55–57

World War I, 2
World War II, 2, 27, 74, 93

Z

Zajde, Nathalie, 39

The manufacturer's authorised representative in the EU is Springer Nature Customer Service Centre GmbH, Europaplatz 3, 69115 Heidelberg, Germany. If you have any concerns regarding our products, please contact ProductSafety@springernature.com

Printed and bound by CPI Group (UK) Ltd, Croydon, CR0 4YY
23/03/2026
02076355-0002